Praise for *Fear, Faith, and a Fistful of Chocolate. . .*

"You've got to love a book that makes you laugh while, at the same time, calming your anxious heart. Worry and Fear have been close friends of mine for way too long; but with Deb's empathetic and funny encouragement, I'm ready to break up with these losers and move on to new friends, Serenity and Peace."
—Becky Johnson, coauthor of *We Laugh, We Cry, We Cook*

"*Fear, Faith, and a Fistful of Chocolate* is a testament to Debora Coty's gift of healing. Once medicated by her quirky humor, we're ready to hear the powerful words she speaks to our touchy, real-world issues."
—Shellie Rushing Tomlinson, Belle of All Things Southern and author of *Sue Ellen's Girl Ain't Fat, She Just Weighs Heavy*

"Debora Coty has written a fresh approach to age-old questions: How do we move past the guilt, doubt, and fear and rely on faith in God for everyday confidence? Her answer: stay fortified with grit, gumption, and Godiva!"
—Edna Ellison, PhD, author of fifteen group studies on friendship

"In authentic Debora Coty style, this book peels back layers of fear everyone deals with and offers practical ways to step out of fear and into freedom. Touching stories of gratitude, compassion, forgiveness, and grace all point us back to ~~the faithful~~ heart and character of our God, who extends His hand to you ~~...~~ because Jesus has faced, experienc~~...~~ won!"
—Jocelyn Hamsher, aut~~...~~ *Fat? Breaking the Cultural M~~...~~ off? Finding Your True Identity in Ch~~...~~*

"*Fear, Faith, and a Fistful of Chocolate* is a delightful book for readers in all walks and stages of life who search for encouragement and wisdom in a fast-paced, competitive, and stress-filled world."
—Anita Corrine Donihue, author of *When I'm on My Knees* and other devotional books

Fear, Faith, and a Fistful of Chocolate

Wit and Wisdom for Sidestepping Life's Worries

Debora M. Coty

BARBOUR
PUBLISHING

In memory of
Suzanne Coty Beatty,
my beloved friend
and sister-in-law,
who demonstrated
by her life and death
how to triumph over fear
with humor, grace,
courage, and faith.

I miss you, Suzi.

- I owe a huge debt of gratitude to the fine folks at Barbour Publishing, especially my editor, Kelly McIntosh, for believing in me enough to make this series happen.

- A big hug to my better-than-triple-chocolate-chunk-brownies agent, Greg Johnson, of WordServe Literary Agency. You da man!

- Boatloads of thanks to the awesome people who were willing to share their hearts and personal fear stories to encourage others: Debbie Cali, Eddie Aiken, Marianna Enlow, Elizabeth Flanagan, Kathleen Taylor, the late Jo Anne Whale, Sandi and Bob Dorey, George Davis, Cheryl Johnston, Don Neel, Patsy Clairmont, Amanda Fort, Teresa Richmond, Lynn Agnew, Rebecca M., Andie Hardee, Nancy Stoppelcamp, Esther Hardy, and Cricket, Josh, and Blaine Boyer.

- Much appreciation to fellow authors who contributed quotes and chapter title ideas: Ronni Scott, Karen Shade, Sarah Biggs-Wudel, and Sharron Cosby.

- Special thanks to all the terrific women who participated in my fear survey and to Carly Johnson for compiling the survey data.

- Undying love and gratitude to my husband, hero, head cheerleader, scripture consultant, and secret chocolate-stash provider, Chuck.

- As always, my heartfelt thanks and praise to Papa God, who truly does make all things possible, even for lily-livered gals terrified of writing a book about fear.

Contents

Introduction 9

Section 1: Internal Fears
Refusing to Water the Wallflower

    1. I'm a Lean, Mean, Frightened Machine
        (Exposing Fear) 14

    2. Vultures Circling My Roof (Humiliation) 20

    3. Soul-Suckers (Rejection) 26

    4. Had Your Vitamin G Today? (Guilt) 34

    5. Single Scoop (Loneliness) 43

Section 2: External Fears
Refilling Mama Bear When the Stuffing's Been
Scared Plum-Out

    6. Who Wants to Be a Wart, Anyway?
        (Curbing Worry) 56

    7. Look, Sure, but Don't Forget to Leap
        (Taking Risks) 65

    8. This Is Only a Test (Anxiety) 75

    9. Hung Up (Controlling Obsessions) 85

    10. Do They Make Prune Smoothies?
        (Uptight about Aging) 98

Section 3: The War Is On
Protecting Ourselves with the Armor of God

11. Chain Mail: The New Silk
    (Underwear of Truth: Gratitude). 111

12. Steel Camisole
    (Breastplate of Righteousness: Compassion) . . . 121

13. Is There a Cure for People Hangovers?
    (Boots of Peace: Forgiveness) 129

14. Fear Not Tomorrow. . .God's Already There
    (Shield of Faith: Perseverance) 140

15. This Helmet Is Worth Hat Hair
    (Helmet of Salvation: Grace) 149

16. Stained-Glass Warrior
    (The Sword of the Spirit: God's Word) 156

Section 4: Faceless Fears
Bogeymen Love the Dark

17. Life after Financial Death (Money). 168

18. Creaks in the Night (Fear of the Unknown) 178

19. Muzzling the Monster (Death) 189

20. Toxic Voices (Detox for Negative Self-Talk) 196

21. Flip On the Light (The Bogeyman's Busted) 207

22. Grit, Gumption, and Godiva (Wrap-Up). 215

Introduction

$\mathcal{D}$o you find yourself hocking up anxiety over and over like a Guernsey regurgitating her cud? Does insecurity nail your feet to the floor? Are you secretly scared that if you stop worrying, your world will fall apart? Do the what-ifs suck joy out of your very soul? Does thinking of the future make your blood run cold?

If you answered yes to any of those questions, you're in good company. Welcome to the sisterhood of weary worrywarts. But, hey, who wants to be a wart?

In my travels as a speaker, I've encountered countless women like me who have spent years running from their own personal fear monsters. Some fears have names and specific countenances; others are faceless, frightening creatures that lurk in the shadows just out of sight. But we know they're there. We *feel* them. And we yearn to boldly step up to those fear monsters and yank off their masks.

That's why I wrote *Fear, Faith, and a Fistful of Chocolate*. It's time we treat fear like the unwanted gift it is and exchange it at heaven's customer service desk for something we can really use: power, love, and self-discipline.

To pinpoint real fears women struggle with on a daily basis, I conducted a survey of 500 random women between the ages of 18 and 80. Here are the top ten fears in descending order:

1. Loss of loved one (spouse/children/parents)
2. Debilitating or terminal disease/illness
3. Failure

   4. Old age/senility
   5. The unknown/the what-ifs
   6. Loneliness
   7. Dependency on others
   8. Rejection
   9. Specific critters (e.g., snakes, roaches, rats)
   10. Being judged unfairly

Within these pages, we'll address these fears (along with others) and explore the reasons they can keep us stretched tighter than size 8 jeans over a size 12 tushie.

I've got to tell you, fear is a scary topic for a humorist. Ain't nothing funny about fear. But there was no mistaking my divine directive from the Boss to tackle it, so you'll find this book a smidge different from my first two books in this "Take On Life" series, *Too Blessed to Be Stressed* and *More Beauty, Less Beast*.

Oh, there will be plenty of the great personal stories bringing scripture to life, which you've told me you love, plus snippets of my quirky humor, and lots of lighthearted but heavy-hitting practical tips. But at the request of Bible study groups who enjoy using these books, I've added a few additional reflection questions (titled More Pluck, Less Chicken) at the end of each chapter, the content of which will be a mite longer and perhaps more serious in tone.

Because fear is serious. And in no way do I wish to trivialize or downplay the destructive force fear often has in our lives. It's real. It's powerful.

But the hope-filled news is there's something even more powerful. Someone, actually, who can break the hold fear has over us. Someone who offers us freedom from fear-a-phobia. "I sought the LORD, and He answered me, and delivered me from all my fears" (Psalm 34:4 NASB).

Our fears spotlight what matters to us most. . .those hidden corners of our life in which we trust Papa God the least. Those are the hot spots we need to work on, girlfriend. Because if we relinquish control to the only One who can truly defeat fear, the thing that scares us to death can be the very thing that propels us to life.

Section 1:
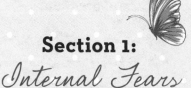

Internal Fears

Refusing to Water the Wallflower

❧

I give you peace,
the kind of peace
that only I can give.
It isn't like the peace that
this world can give.
So don't be worried or afraid.

JOHN 14:27 CEV

Chapter 1

I'm a Lean, Mean, Frightened Machine
(Exposing Fear)

*We will not fear when earthquakes
come and the mountains crumble into the sea.*

PSALM 46:2 NLT

*R*emember the hilarious scene in the movie *Patch Adams*, when Robin Williams's Patch character began to empathize with his roommate's bizarre squirrel phobia? At first Patch couldn't grasp such a nonsensical fear. "They're squirrels," he deadpanned when his bladder-bursting roommate was pinned, terror-stricken, to his bed, believing that invisible rodents had invaded his room.

Patch simply could not connect with this anxiety-riddled guy. Pointing out the absurd didn't work. Logic didn't work. Common sense didn't work. Raw, unexplainable fear trumped them all.

In a flash of enlightenment, Patch finally understood that the only way to help his friend was to enter into his fear with him. To penetrate his personal war zone—as crazy as it seemed (who better than Robin Williams to do crazy?)—and battle fear on its own terms. So during a frenzy of overturned furniture, squirrel nukes, and air bazookas, Patch was able to secure the road to the latrine and provide real, tangible help to someone who was unable to conquer the enemy by himself.

That's exactly why we're here, girlfriend. . .to fall in alongside each other, grab an Uzi, and blow the nuts out of the invisible squirrels that plague each of us.

Those squirrels, of course, come in all shapes and sizes. Some are flesh and blood—people, or specific critters that give us the heebie-jeebies, like snakes, rats, or cockroaches (shudder). Others are without actual bodies but just as real, such as fear of losing our spouse or children, dread of debilitating or terminal illness, and terror of heights or closed spaces. And then there are those ominous, formless fears that swirl around in the dark closets of our minds, filling us with insecurity about the unknown, the future, or things we don't understand.

Five Categories of Everyday Fears

Now I realize that fear is a deep well, and I'm not a professional well driller. But I am a deft (some might say daft) bucket-dipper, and I've worked closely with the side effects of fear during my three decades as a health-care professional. I've learned a few things through study and observation. There are as many different fears as there are belly buttons in this world; but for the sake of simplicity, I've grouped common fears women face into five basic categories, all beginning with the letter *S* (we'll be referring back to these later):

- Spurting fear: An impulsive reaction to a provoking stimulus. Not unlike blood spurting from a fresh puncture wound. This is naked emotion, sister. The unpremeditated, gut-level, internal reaction incited by something that makes us break out in a cold sweat, quiver like a tower of Jell-O, and maybe even toss our cookies. Usually based on previous experience, this type of fear causes us to dutifully avoid things like high ledges, speaking in front of crowds, and confrontation with that sassy-mouthed coworker.

- Savory fear: The delicious thrill elicited by being scared by a specific controlled thing or event. This is an intentional, emotion-driven, temporary fear that we subject ourselves to because we know there's no real danger (or damage) involved. It's fear within the parameters of our safety zones, like riding roller coasters, driving fast, or entering a House of Horrors. Savory means "to give flavor to; to season," and most of us sprinkle little savory fears throughout our lives just because we enjoy the flavor. Hey, we need a cold-chill thrill now and then to remember we're alive!

- Saturating fear: The invasive kind of fear that often originates in childhood and permeates our lives in ways we don't always see. I don't consider saturating fear a conscious emotive response, but equate it with the "spirit of fear" (2 Timothy 1:7 KJV) that the apostle Paul spoke of in his very personal letter from prison to his spiritual son, Timothy, shortly before Paul was beheaded. Saturating fears are probably the hardest to eradicate because they soak into our personalities and become so enmeshed in the fiber of our being, we have difficulty recognizing their individual threads. We don't like them, but we learn to live with them. Sort of like those muffin tops spilling over the waistbands of our jeans. We cover them up or excuse them, telling ourselves, "That's just the way I am," rather than viewing them as something that could potentially be changed.

- Simmering fear: The fear of the unknown, of things we've never experienced but have developed an underlying dread of based on other people's experience and our own speculation. Included in this category would be fear of the future, the infernal what-ifs, dependency on others, loss of employment or possessions, debilitating illness, and the great unknown, death.

- Sovereign fear: Born of respect, this is the subjection under which we willingly place ourselves to those in authority, such as our parents, teachers, spouse, pastor, bosses, and above all, our Creator. Did you know there are over one hundred scriptures advising us to "fear God"? Oh, not in the tremble-from-head-to-toe, wet-your-pants sense, but through awe and respect due to the sovereign, powerful, almighty Commander of our universe.

More about each of these later, but the point I want to make for now is that all fears are not created equal. And they're not all bad.

Sphincter-Pucker Moments

*N*ot long ago, while my fam was chilling at our remote mountain cabin, I took my four-wheeler, Sir Lancelot, out for a spin. Lance is a loud fellow, let me tell you, especially with his propensity for tooting/backfiring/flatulence—whatever term your delicate sensibilities prefer (hence his name, because he has flatu-lance a lot).

Anyway, as I approached the paved road I had to cross to get to the creek-hugging dirt trail on the neighboring mountain, I braked Lance to a rolling stop. A rolling stop—not exactly a full stop. Now, mind you, there was no stop sign (so I wasn't breaking the law), and this particular road had relatively little traffic. But it was on the crest of a steep hill, so that cars nosing up the hill from the right could suddenly appear about ten yards away, and traffic coming from the left could startle you spitless as they careened around the curve.

The saving grace was that in the sound-carrying mountains, you could hear them coming and not do anything stupid.

Unless you were straddling an earsplitting, flatulent ATV.

I glanced right. Nothing coming. So I craned my neck left to peer around the curve as Lance rolled slowly into the highway. Suddenly, a deep rumble rattled my teeth, and I jerked around to find the metallic grill of a huge truck bearing down on me from my right.

Fear actually saved my life. In the three seconds between the time that truck appeared and almost immediately rolled its mammoth wheels across the spot I had just inhabited, panic shot incredible strength to my right thumb. I jammed the accelerator lever so hard that Lance leaped straight up in the air like a crazed rodeo bull and bucked us both into a heap on the far shoulder of the road.

And there I sat in a horrified stupor as the truck, horn blasting an almost-too-late rebuke, disappeared around the curve.

Papa God gave us the emotion of fear for good reason. It serves a useful purpose—to motivate us, move us forward, and keep us from making mistakes. Sometimes fear saves us from ourselves. I mean, how often would we have skipped school growing up just because we didn't feel like going, without the disciplining fear of failure? Or how rotund might we become without fear of regaining that twenty pounds we worked so hard to lose? Why else would we faithfully squash our bosom buddies flat with mammograms without the possibility of that frightening C word invading our bodies? We could be out pounding the pavement if fear of losing our jobs didn't motivate us to get our reports in on time.

It's when fear becomes controlling that it debilitates. When it evolves from an emotion to a *paradigm* (a fifty-cent word that means "worldview"). When it alters our course from the splendid women Papa God intended us to be and makes us settle for a wimpy, whiny imitation. When it begins to dictate our thoughts and behavior.

First fear worms its way into our thinking processes, then it affects our actions. Fear is passion in a negative direction. If we allow fear to continue to wreak havoc in our lives unimpeded, it can eventually erode our self-esteem, relationships, and even our faith.

Okay—are we ready to recognize our enemy for what it really is? Let's dump over a table for cover, get down on our bellies, and do our best GI Jane crawl Patch-Adams style. Time to join forces, clean our weapons of warfare, and blast us some invisible squirrels, girlfriend.

Fear is an acronym in the English language for "False Evidence Appearing Real."

NEALE DONALD WALSCH

More Pluck, Less Chicken

1. What would you say are your biggest fears in the spurting (impulsive reaction) category?

2. The savory (fun, thrilling) category?

3. How about saturating (invasive) and simmering (underlying) fears?

4. Would you say you have a healthy sovereign (respectful) fear of Papa God? How do you show it?

5. Which controlling fears are you currently struggling with? Would you like to loosen their grip on you?

Chapter 2

Vultures Circling My Roof
(Humiliation)

*The fear of public disgrace never
forced me to keep silent.*

JOB 31:34 CEV

∼◦∼

*D*uring one of my many prayer walks around my subdivision,
I couldn't help but notice that one of my neighbors had a
vulture infestation. That's right—a whole herd (gaggle? flock?
committee?) of vultures had taken to lining up across the peak of
his roof.

Now, vultures aren't cute like sparrows or doves; they're huge,
hulking predators with scary, hungry eyes, daggerlike talons, and
ominous, sharp beaks that could rip a body to shreds. And often do.

The thing is, vultures eat dead things. They're raptorial birds
that subsist almost entirely on carcasses. So what in the world are
those vultures waiting around here for? They wouldn't be hanging
around if there wasn't plenty to eat. They'd take off for deader
pastures.

The more I thought about it, I began to wonder if maybe
I don't have vultures on my own roof. Oh, not the beak-and-
feathers kind, but lowlife, spiritual predators. Fearmongers
lurking over my shoulder because I keep them well fed with dead
stuff. I discard tons of decomposing debris. . .failed relationships,

half-cocked ideas that never came to fruition, incomplete projects, abandoned dreams and hopes, good spiritual intentions gasping their last breaths. Rotting, all of them.

A vulture's smorgasbord of demise, dissolution, and decay.

Yep, they're up there all right. I'm sure of it. Hovering, waiting to humiliate me by picking at the bones of my failures. To remind me—and the rest of the world—that I blew it. Again.

But I don't want them stalking me anymore, biding their time until I falter at something else so they can swoop down and sink in their blood-smeared, vulture-y claws. I'm tired of feeling paralyzed, afraid to do anything for fear of doing it wrong.

Can you identify?

I believe that most women, at some point in their lives, are assaulted by the saturating fear of humiliation. Of being completely embarrassed. You may be there right now, wrestling with the nagging, colon-knotting worry that you won't fit in. That you'll look foolish. Or ignorant. Or *different*. That you'll be laughed at, shamed, or ridiculed for something over which you have no control.

And that's the bottom line, isn't it? Fear is really about losing control. About things over which we feel powerless sneaking up and whacking us over the head. Things looming in our future, taking shape in the present, or haunting us from the past. Things we might not even be aware of. Things that make us act a certain way for no apparent reason. It's true—sometimes our adult behavior is influenced by unconscious fears from past events that affect the habits, quirks, and perspectives we have today.

Ghosts from the Past

Take my hat fetish, for example. I've worn hats for decades and never really considered why my closet looks like the Cat in the

Hat exploded. . .stacks of hats everywhere, clogging wall hooks and overflowing shelves. I just thought I liked hats.

Some women are shoe fanatics or fingernail buffs; I'm a hat girl. I can no more pass up a cute hat than Lady Gaga can pass up a lingerie sale.

But something happened recently that opened my eyes to the real, vulture-induced reason for my headwear addiction. It all started so innocently. I posted a Facebook comment about my kicky new fedora, and a childhood school chum, Vicki, responded with an out-of-the-blue question: "Just curious, Deb—are you the daughter who never remembered to brush her hair? I started carrying a brush in my purse after your mom (my teacher at the time) told our health class how important it was to keep your hair neat. She mentioned a daughter that she always had to remind of this. . . . Was it you?"

All of a sudden, I was transported back in time, like a scene from a Stephen King movie, to middle school. I began reliving, in writhing agony, a humiliating memory I had apparently blocked. I was a dorky sixth grader at the time and couldn't have cared less what I looked like. There were so many better things for a rough-and-tumble tomboy to think about—hitting home runs, riding my bike, torturing my sister—it simply never occurred to me to glance in a mirror when I wasn't brushing my teeth.

On this particular day, I had quietly slipped into the back of my mother's health classroom to stick something—I don't remember what—in her purse. The students' backs were facing me and I was tiptoeing while holding my breath, trying so hard not to draw attention to myself while Mama was up front teaching.

Suddenly, Mama stopped in the middle of her hygiene lecture and told everyone to turn around and look at my tousled hair as "an example of poor grooming habits." They were seventh graders—a whole year older than me—and I didn't know any of them, so I was absolutely mortified. And horror of all horrors, there were at least ten *boys* in that class. Gulp. I ducked my head and dashed out the door just as the first giggles began to roll across the room.

Forty years later, sitting in my computer chair, reliving this painful ordeal, my face flamed and I wanted to crawl beneath my desk. In retrospect, as a mother myself, I realized that Mama hadn't meant to hurt me, just jolt me into listening to an admonition I'd ignored a hundred times. She was trying to mold me into a human being instead of a gorilla. My head understood. But my heart still felt that gut-searing shame like the embarrassing episode had just happened.

The long-repressed memory seemed to roll up the shades in my brain and beam light into a corner that's been dark most of my life. All of a sudden the angels sang that full-bodied, eight-note "Ahhhh" chord that means something important just happened.

What an epiphany! I finally got it! I've never been able to explain why I continue to wear, year after unfashionable year, those "embarrassing" hats that my kids used to beg me to hide when their friends were around. Why I just *have* to buy every perky bonnet I see. Why I once chose to leave a basketball game rather than remove my hat when informed that headgear was not allowed in the gym.

My hat fetish was really those nasty vultures all along— those despicable spirit-eaters hovering over my shoulder, threatening further humiliation, and doing their durndest to build a nest in my hair.

So how am I to rid myself of these fear marauders whose circling shadows make embarrassment feel inevitable?

My clue to how to defeat the spiritual vultures came from

the real vultures infesting my neighbor's property. As I crossed the lawn to get a closer look at their rooftop hangout, the hideous creatures first stared me down and spread their wings to threaten me. When I stood my ground, they flew away. My presence frightened them. Vultures aren't intimidated by lifeless carrion, but pit them against a vibrant life force and they're overwhelmed. Outclassed. Outta here.

Then it occurred to me: That's it! That's how we get rid of our spiritual vultures, too—we seek help from the biggest, most powerful life force there is. Those unseen carnivores bringing us down can't remain in His presence. They're totally intimidated. . . overwhelmed. . .outclassed. They're outta here.

"The Spirit who lives in you is greater than the spirit who lives in the world" (1 John 4:4 NLT). That, dear sister, is the difference between an unholy spirit and the Holy Spirit. One has a BB gun and the other has an AK-47. And the Enforcer is on our side.

Spiritual warfare in a nutshell.

I have a feeling your next question is, "So, Deb, are you still wearing hats?" The answer is yes, but not out of compulsion anymore. When I don the plucky Princess Kate number I bought in England (my, oh my, don't those Brits do hats right!), I hold my head high, smile with confidence, and never glance over my shoulder for hungry, winged predators.

Because I know who has my back. And He's packing some heat.

So. . .are there any vultures lurking around your roof? I know a great Exterminator.

Scalded cats fear even cold water.

THOMAS FULLER

More Pluck, Less Chicken

1. Have you been harassed by any vultures (fear of humiliation) lately?

2. In what ways have they tried to build a nest in your hair?

3. Are there any events from your past that cause you to fear failure and shame today?

4. What do you plan to do about it?

5. Backtrack a few paragraphs and reread 1 John 4:4 aloud. Now say it again, this time without looking. Would you accept my challenge to memorize this awesome verse? It's short, incredibly sweet, and the best ammo there is against spiritual vultures.

Chapter 3

Soul-Suckers
(Rejection)

Never will I leave you;
never will I forsake you.

<small>HEBREWS 13:5 NIV</small>

❧

$\mathcal{M}$y friend Philip is one of those perfectionists who, if I didn't love him almost as much as frozen Snickers, would drive this domestic disaster off her nut. You truly could lick Philip's garage floor and feel as though you'd just savored the delicate flavor of clotted cream.

I'm the only living human who has ever eaten in Philip's car. That's simply because I was ornery enough to ignore his stone tablet–chiseled No Food commandment and sneak in a forbidden granola bar to chomp with lip-smacking gusto. Funny, I've never seen anybody's ears turn that shade of maroon. (Strangely enough, the next time I climbed onto Philip's backseat, it was swathed in towels!)

But what's not funny is the chronic inner pressure that drives Philip to painstakingly keep every single one of his possessions in top-notch condition—from his perfectly manicured lawn to his spotless toothbrush and pristine car engine. Why does he scrub the kitchen floor on his knees before work every morning and spend every free moment spit-shining his chrome?

Because Philip feels they are a direct reflection of his self-worth. He's the first to admit that he's fallen into the black hole of investing endless hours, energy, and money in stuff-maintenance. Sometimes at the expense of the people he loves.

Now, I've known a lot of neat freaks, but none quite so, um... well, the word *anal* comes to mind, as Philip. And his perfectionist tendencies translate to work performance and relationships as well. (I still can't figure out why he's friends with me, the gal who grows algae in her vegetable crisper and collects dust bunnies.)

So when I started writing this book about fear, my questions to Philip were: What's at the bottom of your burning need for faultlessness? What are you afraid of?

"I think my perfectionism was fueled by my father's rejection of me as a child," Philip conceded after much soul-searching. "My parents divorced when I was three, and Dad moved to another state. He had little to no contact with me during the years I grew up, and literally turned his back and walked away when he saw me entering the funeral home for my grandmother's [his dad's mother's] funeral."

Wow. That kind of memory weighs heavy on a boy's heart.

But Philip has more. "To say that I felt rejected would be an understatement. Because of his disapproval, I felt the only way I could be accepted was to be good...to be better than good... to be perfect. To excel at everything I did, because then people would respect me. My self-esteem became centered around the things I could do well. If Dad didn't love me, maybe others would because of my accomplishments."

Yet Philip is quick to add that perfectionism is a cruel taskmaster. "Whatever you do, whatever job or undertaking you complete, no matter how well it turns out, you find all the petty faults in it and subsequently translate it into failure. You're never satisfied with your performance, and you begin to view the world with an eye for errors. You focus on the lackluster performance of others and are constantly disappointed when they don't live up to your unrealistic expectations."

This, of course, can result in some hairy relationship moments. Thankfully, Philip has a patient and understanding wife and children who love him dearly, and a heavenly Father he has looked to since his youth as his real Daddy.

"I realize that I'm whole and acceptable to God because of the redeeming work that was done on the cross by Christ. No amount of striving, no passion for perfection, no accomplishment of mine will ever measure up to God's standard of sinless behavior. So if God has already paid the price, and loves me enough to send His Son to die for me, why do I need to struggle so hard trying to be accepted by others when I already have total acceptance by God? It's an easy concept, but one that I must remind myself of over and over again."

The Bottom Line: I'm Not Good Enough

Many of us are perpetually striving to measure up. I never really understood there was a connection with an underlying fear of rejection, but now I get it. Philip's example might be a bit extreme, but all of us have experienced painful rejection in our lives. Perhaps it was from a parent we could never please, a teacher or coach for whom our best just wasn't enough, friends who dropped us, lovers who betrayed us, or employers who pointed us to the door.

Yes, there are definitely soul-suckers out there who drain our confidence and leave us hog-tied with thick ropes of perceived unworthiness.

The fear of disapproval self-perpetuates. To avoid it, we can become obsessive and controlling. We may reject others before they have a chance to reject us. We might even withdraw to protect ourselves. In effect, we reject ourselves by bits and pieces and hide behind masks to feel accepted. We don't know how to be our authentic selves and in the end may become lonely, bitter, or self-loathing.

Do you see yourself in any of these possible scenarios? I think most of us do.

So how do we deal with it? How do we pick ourselves up off the floor after experiencing heart-wrenching rejection? Or gather enough gumption to be our authentic selves around those whose disapproval we dread? Or venture from the emotional closet in which we're hiding to avoid not fitting in?

These are a few awesome ideas I learned from Philip and others who are successfully sparring with the rejection monster:

- Deal with your anger. Acknowledge that it's there, even if it's buried deep beneath layers of denial. If you've thought something like, *This situation is so not right*, or *I was judged unfairly*, or *I wonder how he'd feel if I treated him like swamp rot!*, chances are good that deep down inside, you're irate. But maybe you think it's not "Christian" to be indignant, or you've become proficient at stuffing your animosity. Listen, girlfriend, if you've been rejected and just can't seem to get over it, anger is most likely at the root of your festering wound. It's time to heal that nasty thing so that you're no longer afraid of feeling vulnerable and exposed. Remember, it's not a sin to feel mad. Injustice is supposed to make Christ-followers bristle into action. But anger can evolve into resentment, bitterness, or destructive rage if you don't defuse it. And that, most definitely, is sin. "Go ahead and be angry. You do well to be angry—but don't use your anger as fuel for revenge. And don't stay angry. . . . Don't give the Devil that kind of foothold in your life" (Ephesians 4:26–27 MSG).

- Accept yourself. Recognize that you are not defined by what you do, but by whom Papa God ultimately designed you to be. And remember, you're a work in progress. Your actions do not dictate who you are and whether or not you're acceptable to Him. You are! Philip said it well: "Your self-esteem is not derived from your performance or how nice your car, or house, or even your body looks. Your self-worth comes from the One who created you, and He's already shown you what He thinks of you by sending His beloved only Son to die in your place." That's how important you are, dear sister. C'mon now, get it through your head: You are unique! You're one of a kind! You're "fearfully and wonderfully made" (Psalm 139:14 NASB). Author Elbert Hubbard said, "The greatest mistake you can make in life is to be continually fearing that you will make one." Lighten up. It's okay to be imperfect.

- Don't blow things out of proportion. People with a history of rejection tend to read more rejection between the lines of simple, innocent everyday transactions. Your friend is not abandoning you just because she's too busy to go with you to the concert. Your boss very likely isn't about to fire you simply because he asked you to proofread your report. Okay, take a deep breath. Now exhale. Acknowledge that Papa God is in control and that your petty worrying will not change a single thing. "Who of you by worrying can add a single hour to your life? Since you cannot do this very little thing, why do you worry about the rest?" (Luke 12:25–26 NIV). Overinflating every balloon into a spy dirigible will only make you explode.

- Understand that you are wanted. Cherished. Loved without limits. Wanted. At this moment, you may feel abandoned, or forsaken, or betrayed, but feelings are not trustworthy and can change at the drop of a rogue hormone. Now is the time to overrule your heart with your head. Soften those calloused, scar-encrusted feelings by taping this undying truth to your bathroom mirror or car dashboard and read it aloud daily. See how intimately your Papa God knows and adores you?

  > *You watched me as I was being formed in utter seclusion, as I was woven together in the dark of the womb . . . . How precious are your thoughts about me, O God. They cannot be numbered! I can't even count them; they outnumber the grains of sand! And when I wake up, you are still with me!*
  >
  > PSALM 139:15, 17–18 NLT

  You've gotta love that last line! He's still with you even though He knows you better than anyone in the entire world: inside out, failures and successes, rotten habits and weird quirks. He will not ever leave you. He's absolutely dedicated to you!

- Work on your self-esteem. People with little confidence often struggle with fear of rejection. "After all," they reason, "I'm so pathetic; I don't blame anyone for disrespecting me. I don't even respect myself." But you know what? You don't have to buy that crock. Sure, everybody has weaknesses, but everybody has strengths, too. Yep, even you. Now stop rolling your eyeballs and sassing me under your breath. There's no future in arguing with words on a page. Find out what your strengths and talents are; assess your spiritual gifts and dominant personality traits (Google "personality tests"—there are tons of choices). Ask your pastor, spouse, or a trusted friend to review the results with you and identify your strengths. Now focus your energies for service in these areas; set yourself up for success. For instance, if you're strong in administrative skills, don't sign up to be a volleyball coach. Try women's activities coordinator. If you're good with children, touch a young heart through children's ministry. When you find your niche, you'll feel great about yourself, and you'll also feel Papa God's warm, encouraging smile.

- Chuck the chumps. Go for it. Past failure doesn't dictate future failure. Ever hear, "You can't do that; it's impossible"? This world is full of those who discourage rather than encourage. If we listen to them, we'll never do anything. If we truly believe that God has called us for a particular purpose, we'll keep going for it despite our track record. Author Frank Peretti was turned away by dozens of publishers before his faith-charging books *This Present Darkness* and *Piercing the Darkness* took the world by storm and drew tens of thousands to their knees. What if he had stopped trying after the nineteenth rejection? What if you stop after yours?

- Listen to the right voice. We all have those little voices speaking over our shoulders: the wise voice and the stupid voice. The wise voice says, "It's okay to like yourself. . .after all, God is proud of you—you're one of His faves." The stupid voice counters with, "You're a worthless loser; who could possibly like you?" The wise voice suggests, "Get to know Papa God better through prayer and His Word." The stupid voice says, "Just keep doing what you've been doing; nothing will ever change anyway." The wise voice whispers, "Invest yourself in relationships, not stuff that will only rust and decay; make precious lasting memories with those you love." The stupid voice shouts, "People are too risky. They'll only dump you when they get to know the real you. Buy another flashy car and don't let any messy women authors anywhere near it." So which voice do you choose to listen to?

*There is no one alive
who is Youer than You.*

DR. SEUSS

More Pluck, Less Chicken

1. Has anything in your childhood contributed to feelings of rejection as an adult?

2. What tactics do you use to avoid disapproval from others?

3. Do you have any unresolved anger issues related to past or recent rejections? What steps will you take to deal with them?

4. Do you tend to overinflate worry balloons into dirigibles? How can you keep the Hindenburg from floating around inside your head at night?

5. What are the kinds of things the wise voice on your shoulder whispers to you? How about your stupid voice? Which do you tend to listen to?

Chapter 4

Had Your Vitamin G Today?
(Guilt)

How far has the Lord taken our sins from us?
Farther than the distance from east to west!

PSALM 103:12 CEV

*M*y friend George was throwing a party. Not a huge wingding, but a nice birthday get-together for a group of close friends and relatives. Bethany, his friend and business assistant, couldn't be there, but graciously offered her secluded home on the river for the weekend while she was out of town.

George and his wife, Sara, arrived at Bethany's house Saturday to prepare for the party and to stay overnight to take care of Bethany's beloved cats. When the guests arrived, George and his brother-in-law Neil decided to sharpen their archery skills at the target set up out back.

I need to make it clear at this point in the story that we're talking about an attorney and a psychiatrist here. George and Neil are both highly educated, respectable men. . .prominent community, business, and church leaders. I say that now because you might not believe it after the next few paragraphs.

Everything went well with target practice at first, until George shot an arrow that ricocheted off the edge of the target and disappeared into the high grass. A high-pitched yowl suddenly rent the air, and the men stood horrified as Bethany's cat Muffin stumbled into the clearing, skewered completely through by George's arrow. The feathered shaft of the arrow protruded from one side of Muffin while the pointy side stuck out the other like an old Steve Martin sight gag. Only this wasn't funny.

Now, not to worry if you're a bit squeamish at this point. Believe it or not, this true story has a happy ending.

But at the moment, George and Neil were appalled. What to do? It would tank the party if they lugged a speared cat inside. Although Muffin was still alive—and pretty ticked off—she was losing blood, and the men had no clue how to remove the arrow. It couldn't be pulled out without causing more damage. The arrowhead would have to be sawed off and the feathered shaft backed out.

While someone held down an angry, wounded cat.

Nope. Not going to happen. You're cringing right now if you've ever tried to bathe a healthy cat, much less do surgery on a cat-on-a-spit without anesthesia.

It seemed obvious that Muffin couldn't possibly live, shish-kabobbed as she was. Should they put her out of her misery? Wait for her to bleed to death? Call 911?

Finally, the guys decided to keep the cat-kabob dilemma under wraps. Nobody needed to know. The plan was to let Muffin just continue to lie where she was, dig a hole at the edge of the woods, and bury her as soon as she kicked the bucket. It would appear as if she'd run away. Don't cats do that all the time?

So they found a shovel and started digging. When the hole was finished, they went back for Muffin. But whoops! Muffin was gone. What? Gone? Where could she possibly go with a two-foot-long arrow protruding from her middle? They sure didn't want one of the children to find an impaled cat, so the coconspirators combed the whole area but. . .no Muffin. Anywhere.

All through dinner, the two guys covertly kept an eye on the yard, expecting Muffin to stagger up at any minute and let the cat out of the bag (sorry—couldn't resist the snarky pun!). But she didn't. Ironically, Muffin's feline twin took a strange liking to George, rubbing against his legs and attempting to cuddle in his lap the entire meal, prompting one of the guests to comment, "George, you sure have a way with cats."

He nearly choked.

After dinner, George and Neil sneaked back outside for one final search before nightfall. Nothing. But still they kept their dark secret.

Neil and the other guests left later that evening, and George began to sweat despite the cold front that dropped the temperature into the low twenties. How would he ever explain this to Bethany? He peeked out the blinds into the darkness as he helped Sara clean up. But he just couldn't force himself to confess, even when Sara brought the other cats in for the night and kept calling and calling the missing Muffin, fretting over where she could possibly be. "It's freezing tonight; what will poor little Muffin do? Bethany will never forgive us if anything happens to her baby."

So as you can well imagine, George endured a restless night. At the first crack of dawn, he threw on his coat and jeans and crept outside, expecting to locate and bury the frozen evidence of his guilt before anyone was the wiser.

But what he found shocked his socks off.

First there was a bloodstained arrowhead lying on the frosty ground, and then a few yards farther, the rest of the arrow—the feathered shaft—completely intact. Then, lo and behold, there was Muffin herself, curled up and sleeping peacefully on a soft, warm bed of lichen. . .with a telltale hole in her side and only eight lives remaining.

George knew it was time to confess. The guilt tsunami hit the beach.

Twelve hundred dollars later, the veterinarian assured George and a dazed Bethany that Muffin would be fine. The arrow had miraculously passed just below her spinal column and millimeters above her vital organs. But one mystery remained: How had the arrow been removed? It couldn't possibly have fallen apart on its own, and there was absolutely no way Muffin could have rubbed or pawed the arrowhead off. Hmm. Did Muffin have a guardian angel with a bowl of catnip and a pair of pliers?

I guess we'll never know. Where's Nancy Drew when you need her?

Types of Guilt

Thankfully most of us don't skewer kitties on a regular basis; but, like George, we do choke on our guilt sometimes. Guilt is so hard to swallow. Its effect is kind of like a vitamin in reverse. Instead of nourishing our bodies, it depletes our spirits. And yet we faithfully keep popping that vitamin G (Guilt) every day as if we can't live without it.

Hmm. What would life be like without daily doses of guilt? If you're like me, it's hard to imagine. . . . I've built Mount Everests out of guilt anthills far too long to fathom a nice, smooth, bumpless existence.

Well, for one thing, without daily doses of vitamin G I think we'd definitely be more content. We wouldn't be struggling with either ice cream guilt or I-scream guilt as I describe in my book *More Beauty, Less Beast* (in the chapter "Patching the Leaky Cauldron").

Ice cream guilt is all about behaviors that can and probably should be changed, such as scarfing down a half gallon of Chunky Monkey before bed. (Or attempting to secretly bury a skewered feline.) We know deep inside that we shouldn't be doing it, and the guilt that twangs our conscience is actually a good guilt, a healthy guilt that serves as a catalyst for change.

This type of guilt is basically a fact of life for believers. We should not only expect it, but welcome it. Ice cream guilt sounds the alarm that we've violated God's value system—oh, let's just put on our big girl panties and call it what it is: sin.

Incidentally, did you know that the word *sin* is an ancient archery term meaning "missing the target"? Quite a giggler considering the cat-kabob story, don't you think?

Anyway, ice cream guilt spotlights behaviors and attitudes that need to be dealt with because sin creates a wall between us and Papa God. We can't live—and I mean really live a fulfilling life of abundant joy—if we're separated from our source of sustenance. Can a flower bloom with a broken stem? No, it withers and dies. How long could you subsist if a concrete wall suddenly blocked access to your kitchen—your source of physical sustenance? (Excluding takeout!)

It's the same way when sin blocks the source of our spiritual sustenance. Guilt serves as the motivation for us to take a sledgehammer to that wall, repent of our sin, and change our ways of thinking and acting to better reflect Christ.

Conversely, I-scream guilt is the endless obsession about things completely out of our control to change. For example, causing a car accident that severely injures someone, or feeling convinced that your estrangement from your husband caused your son to turn to drugs. It's the nagging, debilitating, unhealthy guilt that dogs us until we just want to scream. We can't change what happened, but even after we've asked for forgiveness, we still drag around huge, heaping chains of remorse and deep sorrow that have the potential to crush our spirits if we let them.

My friend Esther uses a great mental tool to help her drop I-scream guilt like a maggot-infested carcass and resist ever picking it back up. "Guilt is a dead thing," Esther says, her cinnamon-colored eyes flashing. "If you think of old, already forgiven sin as a dead thing, imagine you're digging it up from its grave every time you revisit it."

Eww. Esther's absolutely right. Who wants to play with a decaying dead thing? We need to leave it buried and move on!

Guilt That Keeps on Taking

But what do we do when, after we repent and ask Jesus for a sledgehammer to take a few swings at that dividing wall, guilt continues to plague us? We may respond in shame, anger, or depression, which only serves as mortar to fortify the wall. It grows even taller and thicker. Soon it becomes the Great Wall of China.

Why won't it stop? Because Satan, the archenemy of our souls, is using our guilt to strengthen that despicable wall and separate us from our Lord. Listen, sister, that's what "the accuser" (the name referring to Satan in Revelation 12:10) does best. He accuses us mercilessly and racks us with guilt that makes us feel worthless and unworthy of Papa God's love. He makes us think we're too bad, too useless, or too far gone for any hope of restoration. We might as well dig a grave and crawl into it. Death couldn't be any worse. Why would the Creator of truth and beauty want to have anything to do with us?

Listen to me right now: It's a lie.

The Accuser underestimates our Savior's mercy. Yes, mercy: that incredibly powerful, wall-obliterating wrecking ball that is Papa God's specialty. The all-encompassing forgiveness and acceptance that led the writer of Romans to proclaim, "There is no condemnation for those who belong to Christ Jesus. And because you belong to him, the power of the life-giving Spirit has freed you from the power of sin that leads to death" (Romans 8:1–2 NLT).

No condemnation. No Accuser. No more guilt. The dividing wall comes a-tumblin' down under the relentless power of the wrecking ball of mercy.

Fly, Fly Away

Do you recall the 1973 classic film *Papillon* (French for "butterfly")? I was moved by it decades ago and just saw it again on TV. I'll never forget one particular scene in that movie, which was based on French convict Henri Charriere's true-life story.

Henri, nicknamed Papillion (played by Steve McQueen), is unjustly convicted of murder and sentenced to incarceration at a hellish penal colony on Devil's Island in French Guyana.

Several ill-fated escape attempts with his prisoner buddy (played by a young Dustin Hoffman) result in year after year of solitary confinement in deplorable conditions. During one stretch of time in complete darkness and nerve-shattering silence, Papillion has a nightmare in which he's brought before an imposing judge and jury.

Judge to Papillion: "You have been accused of the worst crime in all of humanity—a wasted life."

After a long moment of reflection, Papillion, with stricken eyes, replies to his accuser, "Guilty. . . Guilty. . . Guilty. . ." as he slowly turns and dejectedly walks away.

That scene is truly haunting, I think, because it nails one of our deepest fears: a wasted life. Insignificance. Unimportance.

We need to feel that our life is meaningful, that we're achieving some purpose. That no matter what we've done, Papa God can repair, restore, and revitalize the remnants of our lives for His higher glory.

And He can. It's true. Believe it. Then act like you believe it.

Look at our biblical examples: Rahab the harlot, David the murderer, Jacob the deceiver, and Peter the betrayer. All made terrible choices that resulted in heinous sin. Yes, they were guilty. Yet they refused to wallow in guilt over their mistakes. Instead, they rose above the guilt-mire and moved forward in forgiveness to accomplish mighty things for God.

And we can, too. If only we remember that taking action releases guilt; obsessing over the past doesn't.

Sure, it's important to acknowledge guilt when guilt is due. But we don't have to dejectedly walk away from the Accuser with that guilt weighing us down forever. We can be forgiven, redeemed, and rebooted. We may be guilty, but we're not incarcerated in a "guilted" cage. Mercy has unlocked the door.

"Don't you realize that you become the slave of whatever you choose to obey? You can be a slave to sin, which leads to death, or you can choose to obey God, which leads to righteous living" (Romans 6:16 NLT).

I choose to obey God. How about you? Guilt is not my master. Jehovah is the boss of me. The cat's out of the bag. Girlfriend, we've been pardoned!

*You'll be sorry about this
when I'm on my deathbed. . . .*

AUTHOR FAITH MCDONALD'S RENDITION

OF HOW TO GUILT YOUR KIDS

More Pluck, Less Chicken

1. Okay, maybe you're not a cat impaler, but what's one thing you've done that caused your tsunami of guilt to hit the beach?

2. Do you tend to swallow daily doses of vitamin G related to your family? Work? Church? Personal relationship with Papa God? What twangs your conscience most?

3. Can you differentiate between ice cream guilt and I-scream guilt? Which builds the highest wall between you and your Lord? How can you knock that sucker down?

4. Reread Romans 8:1–2 (earlier in this chapter). Now consider Psalm 29:11 (MSG): "GOD makes his people strong. GOD gives his people peace." How do these promises relate to your life? How can Papa God's mercy release you from the Accuser's custody? If you have a copy of *More Beauty, Less Beast,* turn to chapter 15 for additional effective action steps for overcoming guilt.

5. Name three ways in which your life is meaningful . . .important. . .significant. Don't be shy, now—be truthful and proud! How is the Lord using you for His higher glory?

Chapter 5

Single Scoop
(Loneliness)

By yourself you're unprotected.
With a friend you can face the worst.

ECCLESIASTES 4:12 MSG

I looked around in disbelief. I couldn't believe it was happening again. In a huge dining hall teeming with people, I was all alone. And feeling wretched.

I'd just been through the same thing that very morning when I had entered the dining hall a bit early for breakfast. It was the second day of the five-day speakers' conference, and I wanted to get a jump start on the busy schedule. So as soon as the serving line opened, I was one of the early birds fluttering through, settling myself afterward at a large empty table that had been crowded at dinner the night before. I didn't know a soul, and this seemed like a good place to meet a few.

Although dozens of people followed me through the line, not one opted to sit at my table. Not one. So I finished my eggs in isolation, watching small groups gathering at other tables all around the room.

I felt uncomfortable but ignored the unbidden seeds of rejection that planted themselves in my gut. *Don't be silly, Deb.*

It's not personal. You're not an outcast, for heaven's sake. They just happened to sit elsewhere, that's all. Get over it.

But here at lunchtime, it felt like déjà vu. Only worse. Because now it was obvious it wasn't my imagination—something must be wrong with me. This time I had entered the dining hall resolved to join a prepopulated table and not leave my socialization up to chance.

So I approached a table set for ten where two ladies were already seated, chatting happily.

"May I join you?" I asked with a smile.

"Sure," one replied, friendly enough. "Nobody's sitting there," said the other as I strategically placed my plate so I could converse with them both. After I'd fixed my drink and returned to my seat, I silently gave thanks for my meal, smiled again at my potential new girlfriends, and began cutting my meat as they continued talking nonstop. To each other.

At first, I tried to appear interested and engaged while waiting for an appropriate time to enter into the conversation. But it never came. In fact, the woman closest to me actually swiveled in her chair so that she was facing the other woman with her back to me. Ten solid minutes passed. It felt like ten hours. I tried not to look frantic as I scanned the room, trying to make eye contact with someone—anyone—who might be willing to cast a few crumbs of companionship my way.

But everyone was busily eating, talking with their tablemates, or scurrying about, preoccupied with the homework we'd been given.

So there I sat, completely invisible to the pair who laughed and chattered and forged a lively friendship within my arm's reach.

That seed of rejection planted at breakfast sprouted with a vengeance, shot up with lightning speed, and burst into full bloom.

What's wrong with me? Why won't anyone talk to me? Nobody

likes me. That's what it is. Nobody likes me. But they don't know me. I must look weird. Or mean. Do I look mean? Maybe they've all heard that I'm not a nice person and they've decided to avoid me this whole week. All 150 of them. This is horrible. I feel like a leper. I'm a pariah. Maybe I should just stay in my room and skip meals.

Was I thinking rationally? No. Were my thoughts recklessly driven by deep fears and reactive emotions I didn't fully grasp at the moment? Absolutely. Did I—a grown, supposedly mature woman—suddenly rise, leave my half-eaten food on the table, and, blinking back tears, flee to the safety of my room where I had a complete meltdown?

Sadly, yes.

I hate to admit it, but I threw myself on the bed, curled into a fetal ball, and had a snot-flying cry, just like I did as a lonely ten-year-old.

One Is the Scariest Number

We've all experienced times of loneliness, haven't we? I don't mean solitude—there's a distinct difference. We're not lonely every time we're alone; sometimes being alone is a good thing—a time for reflection, for planning, for regenerating. Solitude is a gentle aloneness that's essential for sorting out our thoughts, experiencing emotional healing, getting to know ourselves, and dialing down to listen for the still, small voice of our Lord.

Some of us are alone because we have no family nearby, are widowed, have a difficult time making (or keeping) friends, or simply by choice. Perhaps we're shy or just haven't yet hooked up with a church or community group. Maybe we devote so much time to work, ministry, or staying online that we barely notice we're living solo.

But make no mistake, logging hours e-mailing, blogging,

tweeting, or texting is not the same as actually conversing with people. These modes of current communication technology may make us feel less alone, but connecting is not equal to conversing.

According to psychologist Sherry Turkle,[1] who studies modern communication trends, one of the big reasons technology has become so popular during the last decade is because of our fear of aloneness. Why would anyone sit alone at a meeting, on a park bench, on a bus, at an airport, or anywhere else when they can whip out a smartphone and instantly feel connected to someone?

It doesn't even matter if we're surrounded by friends, family, or children craving our attention; we're still glued to the magical device that feeds the illusion that we're in control and need never be alone. That we can dictate who or what receives our attention and when.

I know what you're probably thinking: *But, Deb, conversation in real time is scary.* You're right—it sure is. We can't edit, tweak, revise, and carefully present ourselves the way we'd prefer to be seen like we can in cyberworld. There, ours is a calculated presence. We're more in command than in real-life conversations when we stumble over our words, accidentally insult people, spray saliva, laugh like a hyena, or say something so stupid we wish we could hit the DELETE button on the whole day.

But that's how we share ourselves with each other. Our real selves. And develop real relationships that include the good, the bad, and the ridiculous. Relationships that celebrate both our adorableness and our absurdity—lasting relationships that truly obliterate loneliness.

Loneliness is not like solitude. It's razor-edged, unwanted aloneness. Loneliness is an unrequited desire to join together, a yearning to share closeness with another beating heart, craving companionship but not being able to have it. Loneliness is feeling like you're the only one on the planet, although you may be surrounded by throngs.

Loneliness tears down our defenses, dismantles our self-esteem, and reduces us to ineffective mush-piles of perceived worthlessness.

Because loneliness is so devastating to us, we fear feeling lonely. And because we fear it, we're at risk of becoming emotional hermits, stealthily avoiding situations where we might be assaulted by the memory of how it felt back in school to be the last one standing when everyone else was chosen for the ball team. Or by the popular crowd. Or by a boyfriend. Or for the honor roll. Or the prom.

When we're that kind of lonely, we're engulfed by shame. Embarrassment. Humiliation. Like we're a pathetic waste of flesh and bone.

But hear me, girlfriend: You're not a pathetic waste of flesh and bone. And neither am I. Papa God—your heavenly Papa—doesn't want you to feel ostracized. . .or exiled. . .or isolated from the rest of His children. He is not into solitary confinement. He's into life and health and heart connections and belly laughs and soul sisters.

They Don't Make a Shot for This

We mustn't give fear the authority to hold us prisoner in our own skin. We don't have to wither away in our silent little cells. No, ma'am, we do not. In order to conquer our fear of loneliness, we need to grow some spunk, pick the lock, and turn RABID:

R: Reach out. Make the initial effort. If you wait on someone else to make the first move, you may be waiting until you're wearing granny undies the size of a pup tent. C'mon now—it's not as scary as you imagine. People don't actually die of civility poisoning. Just try this: First, carefully consider your options. Target someone who interests you and appears seeker-friendly. When she isn't busy or preoccupied (choose the right time, not when she's watching *Dancing with the Stars*), approach her and smile. Sure, there's a risk that your efforts might be rebuffed, but if so, it's her loss. Try again. Your new best friend may be only a "hello" away.

A: Attract, don't repel. Take an honest self-assessment of these socializing basics:

1. Cleanliness: Nobody wants to chat with someone who appears to have rolled in roadkill. How's your breath? Is your hair washed and combed? Do you reek of excessive perfume? Big turnoff. You don't have to exude perfection; just be clean and neat.

2. Friendliness: Do you have a cheerful countenance? Is your expression pleasant and inviting? Is your body language open? Or closed (e.g., arms crossed, head down, eyes flitting around the room or staring at the floor)? Are you speaking too loudly or too softly for the setting? Are you inadvertently coming across as overbearing or pushy? Or maybe jittery as a mouse in a boa pit? Don't expect any doorbells to ring if your Go Away doormat is laid out.

3. Are you actively listening? Remember, it's not about you. When you meet new people, do you tend to talk too much about yourself? Or do you take an active interest in what they're saying? Are you making good eye contact, asking thoughtful questions to clarify what was said, and offering follow-up responses that show concern? Don't listen

passively: "Uh-huh. Uh-huh. Uh-huh." Listen actively: "Really? I'd like to hear more about that."

B: Be proactive. Get moving, do something. Go where people are; don't just lie around moping about your loneliness. Nothing is likely to change about your situation until you become proactive and initiate change. I love the scene in the movie *Notting Hill* when Hugh Grant's character asks his funky roommate, Spike, why he's wearing a wet suit to breakfast. Spike replies, "No clean clothes." And then Hugh's insightful comment: "There never will be unless you actually clean your clothes."

I: Implant scripture. Store some verses in your memory bank so you can retrieve them readily. It will enable you to think rationally as Papa God's words ground your runaway thoughts and will stymie meltdowns. Allow the Holy Spirit to empower you to control your emotions. Here are some of my favorite strong, easy-to-memorize verses:

- "Love your enemies and pray for anyone who mistreats you." (Matthew 5:44 CEV)

- "I will give you a new heart and put a new spirit in you." (Ezekiel 36:26 NIV)

- A gentle tongue can break a bone. (Proverbs 25:15 NIV)

- When I am weak, then I am strong. (2 Corinthians 12:10 NASB)

- Pride lands you flat on your face; humility prepares you for honors. (Proverbs 29:23 MSG)

- When I am afraid, I put my trust in you. (Psalm 56:3 NIV)

- Encourage one another and build each other up. (1 Thessalonians 5:11 NIV)

- "Do not judge, or you too will be judged." (Matthew 7:1 NIV)

- It's smart to be patient, but it's stupid to lose your temper. (Proverbs 14:29 CEV)

- Keep your mouth shut, and you will stay out of trouble. (Proverbs 21:23 NLT)

- If our minds are ruled by our desires, we will die. But if our minds are ruled by the Spirit, we will have life and peace. (Romans 8:6 CEV)

- Don't hit back; discover beauty in everyone. (Romans 12:17 MSG)

- We get knocked down, but we are not destroyed. (2 Corinthians 4:9 NLT)

Whoa, momma, I got started and couldn't stop. Of course, these are just suggestions—there are tons more, but the point is: Choose your own faves and commit them to memory so they can pick you up when you've been knocked down (hey, you can even sing that one!).

D: Develop a plan. And stick to it even when you don't feel like it. Decide ahead of time how you'll react in different scenarios, and don't give up if your first effort fails. Go ahead, girl. . .get RABID!

A Happier Ending

*O*kay, let's revisit my speaking conference fiasco and see how it turned out once I turned RABID.

As I recall, we left me balled up on my bed, sobbing my heart out (I could have avoided all that if I'd only recalled the I in RABID). After the waterfall ebbed, I realized that if I didn't want to spend the rest of the week hiding in my room, painting my toenails, I'd better become proactive.

My self-assessment revealed no major snafus (except a slurpy nose and raccoon eyes from tear-smeared mascara). My confidence rose when I gave myself a little pep talk about being a more experienced speaker than most of the folks at this conference. I didn't need to feel bad about myself—I had a lot to offer the newbies, and they would likely be grateful if I shared my experience and knowledge with them. But only if they asked; I vowed not to push anything on anyone.

Repeating the scriptures I've listed on the previous pages (plus a few others) enabled me to grow stronger with each and every one. God's Word truly is powerful. Trust me—it'll put some starch in your drawers.

So that night, I entered the dining hall with a plan. I carefully scoped out the room and chose a large table that was three-quarters full (if one or even two people didn't work out, there were plenty of other options). I parked myself between a pleasant-looking woman and a man crimson-faced from laughing (a good sense of humor is always promising). Then I briefly introduced myself and began asking open-ended questions (as opposed to yes/no questions): "Where do you call home?" "What do you do for a living?" "What project are you currently working on for tonight's workshop?" I took a real interest and listened to their answers, pointing out things we had in common.

Both of my seatmates were extremely responsive, and we ended up exchanging e-dresses and greeting each other like old buddies throughout the remainder of the conference. Alone times don't feel lonely when you're confident that you have a friend nearby. There is, after all, comfort in companionship: "Someone might be able to beat up one of you, but not both of you" (Ecclesiastes 4:12 CEV).

We weren't meant to go it alone, sister. We don't need another dent in our self-worth fenders. Look at Adam and Eve . . .David and Jonathan. . .Ruth and Naomi. . .Shrek and Donkey. We need relationships, and sometimes it just requires a little resourcefulness—and turning RABID—to find our Donkey.

> *Thinking will not overcome fear,*
> *but action will.*
>
> W. CLEMENT STONE

More Pluck, Less Chicken

1. Donkey had to convince Shrek that having a friend was better than being alone. Many people—including me—value their solitude and are quite protective of it. Would you say you're more of a Shrek or a Donkey when it comes to alone time?

2. Ralph Waldo Emerson said, "Fear defeats more people than any other one thing in the world." How has fear of loneliness affected your behavior in the past? In the present?

3. Which scripture already implanted in your brain is your go-to verse to stymie meltdowns? Do any from the list strike you as a scripture you'd like to add to your arsenal?

4. Review what RABID stands for; which of the tenets do you think will be the simplest for you to implement in fending off loneliness? Which will be the hardest? Why?

5. According to Ecclesiastes 4:10, "If you fall, a friend can help you up. But if you fall without having a friend nearby, you are really in trouble" (CEV). What does this verse say regarding loneliness?

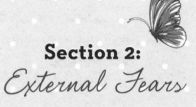

Section 2:
External Fears

Refilling Mama Bear When the
Stuffing's Been Scared Plum-Out

In God I trust and am not afraid.
What can man do to me?

PSALM 56:11 NIV

Chapter 6

Who Wants to Be a Wart, Anyway?
(Curbing Worry)

> *Don't worry about anything;*
> *instead, pray about everything.*
> *Tell God what you need,*
> *and thank him for all he has done.*

PHILIPPIANS 4:6 NLT

*D*on't be such a worrywart," my sister, Cindy, said to me not so long ago. "No wonder you don't sleep well—your worry never turns off."

She was right. Not only was I restlessly churning up the bedsheets half the night, but my constant worrying made me tense and edgy much of the day, too. Can you identify, girlfriend?

As I mentioned in my book *Too Blessed to Be Stressed*, I've spent decades honing my worry skill into the fine-tuned machine it is today. I can whip pesky irritants into frothy, acetic colon-coaters faster than any handy-dandy juicer on the market.

This is not a good thing.

I've come to realize worrying is a form of self-centeredness— it keeps us focused on getting rather than giving, and keeps our eyes on ourselves instead of others. Worriers are preoccupied with protecting themselves. Worry has no redeeming qualities. It never fulfills its promises. Instead, it drains our energy reserves, adds spiderweb wrinkles on our foreheads, and makes us woefully weary.

Worry is a type of simmering fear that doesn't seem like fear at all because it masquerades as taking responsibility. We can easily fool ourselves into thinking we're doing the responsible thing by agonizing over dilemmas. By dwelling on our troubles, we think that we'll somehow become enlightened with magical answers that will change inevitable outcomes. Fretting and stewing and fussing seem perfectly normal because we're so used to it.

But over time, worrying inflates our problems to appear huge. Enormous. Insurmountable. Even bigger than Papa God.

Shocking when you think of it that way, isn't it? That anything could seem bigger than the Creator of heaven and earth? But the bottom line in worrying is a lack of trust that Papa God can—and will—take care of us. We believe we're protecting ourselves by obsessing over what the future might whack upside our head so we won't be taken by surprise. Like good little Girl Scouts, we want to be prepared.

Oftentimes, worry causes us to live in the future instead of the present, looking ahead to anticipate potential problems before they arise. But living in the present—the here and now—is where real life is. Author Leo Buscaglia said, "Worry never robs tomorrow of its sorrow; it only saps today of its joy."

You know, it really is a control issue. By worrying, we're desperately trying to maintain control. We keep our manicured fingernails clutching on to every shred of our lives because underneath it all, we're afraid to relinquish complete control to the Lord. Why? Oh, we both know why, don't we?

Because things might not turn out the way we want them to.

And our guts pay the price for choosing a worrying (aka controlling) lifestyle. After we've "wept a little weep" (an awesome phrase from Louisa May Alcott's *Little Women*), we bury aches, pains, twinges, and jitters with pills, alcohol, absentminded eating, antacids, caffeine, or my sedative of choice, Cadbury chocolate bars (with almonds). Worry drains our joy like water in an unplugged sink. We don't even realize it, but we've chosen the gray crayon to color our world.

Okay, here's the deal: Our bodies and minds were not designed to withstand chronic worry. That's why our stomachs end up with turmoil-gouged ulcers, why mental wards flourish, and why Xanax even exists. An hour of worrying is ten times more exhausting than an hour of work. Proof that worry is not the lifestyle our Creator intends for us: Jesus Himself said as much in Luke 12:26: "If worry can't accomplish a little thing. . . what's the use of worrying over bigger things?" (NLT).

But there's good news. Worry is a learned habit. And since it's learned, it can be unlearned.

How? Well, we have to train our brains to react to troubles in a different way. A calmer, healthier way. A way that colors our world with a rosier crayon.

Anti-Worrywart Tools

*B*ased largely on the scripture at the beginning of this chapter, here are some simple anti-worrywart tools that I find extremely helpful in my own ongoing quest for serenity.

- Postpone worry. Set aside fifteen minutes a day as your designated worry time. Then, whenever a niggling fret worms into your brain during the day or night, jot it down. Now that you've recorded it, you can forget about it and not waste precious living time dwelling on it. One gal said she sets aside a half hour every day to do all her worrying, then she takes a nap during that time. Wise woman!

- Morph worry into prayer. When you do get to that designated worry time, rather than chewing and chewing gristle that won't ever digest, turn each problem into a prayer request and allow your heavenly Father to clean your plate. Fretting is not productive. Prayer is. Prayer is the nerve that innervates the muscles in the hand of God.

- Fire worry. Worry brings zero return on your investment and adds nothing to your portfolio. Channel Donald Trump and send worry packing. Replace it with a busy body. Redirect your thoughts by giving your brain—and body—something else to do. Action defuses anxiety. Author Glenn Turner says, "Worrying is like a rocking chair; it gives you something to do, but it gets you nowhere." When you start to worry, get your hands busy and your mind will follow. Hey, just walk into your kitchen. If yours is like mine, there are always a thousand things that need to be done: scour the green fuzz off the crisper, search for that elusive 2006 frozen rump roast, dismantle Mount St. Chuck in the dish drainer (my husband's quirky habit of trying to win the World Dish-Stacking Championship). And sing along to your favorite music while you're working—music is the best of distractions.

- Go to your happy place. Another gem for worry-redirection, especially late at night when those to-do lists parade through your brain like sheep wearing little electronic signboards flashing reminders for tomorrow. Imagine that you're in that special place that brings you peace and happiness. For instance, plop yourself right on your favorite beach in your mind—feel the salty breeze blowing your hair, hear the foaming surf ebb and flow, dig your toes into the soft, warm sand. Ahh. Feel that anxiety melt away. For me, it's a remote trail above our Smoky Mountain cabin, where I've always experienced the presence of my Creator through His magnificent creation. In a flash, I'm feeling more relaxed.

- Rest in the Word. Another great worry-buster for restless nights when you're more uptight than a twisted thong: Reflecting on a favorite scripture is a wonderful way to bring peace to your soul. Choose a verse, say it aloud, then let it roll through your mind over and over until you can think of nothing else. Some of my nighttime go-to verses are Proverbs 3:5–6, "Trust in the LORD with all your heart and lean not on your own understanding; in all your ways submit to him, and he will make your paths straight" (NIV), and Matthew 11:29, " 'Learn from me, for I am gentle and humble in heart, and you will find rest for your souls' " (NIV). Soak in His gentle ways as His restful Spirit caresses and calms you.

- Exercise intentional gratitude. Anxiety is often the result of counting everyone else's blessings except your own. Gratitude doesn't come naturally to most of us (why is it so much easier to grouse?). . .it's truly an exercise, requiring no less discipline than pumping iron at the gym. We'll talk more about living gratefully in chapter 11, but a good way to start is the Hand Rule: Don't allow yourself to entertain one worry before you count off with the fingers of one hand five things for which to be thankful. As you extend each finger, end with an open hand in a gesture of release to Papa God. Before you know it, your perspective will be more positive.

- Perform emotional triage. Worriers excel at avoiding

unpleasant feelings by keeping their problems at bay in their heads rather than confronting reality and its associated emotions. Sure, it may be terrifying to face that upcoming layoff at work, but constantly stewing about it won't stop it from happening. Conversely, it just might render you proactively impotent in finding another position. Sort your nagging concerns into two piles: those with outcomes over which you have no control, and those that are potentially solvable. Give the first pile to the Lord, turn your back on it, and focus on the solvable problems. Seek guidance, wise advice, and emotional support from trusted friends and family to come up with an action plan. Once you begin following your plan and seeing results, your worry will diminish.

Going on a Fret-Free Diet

Are you still having a hard time believing there's any other way than the lifestyle of worrying you've always known? Perhaps that's all you ever saw your momma do, and maybe your grandma, too. A worry-free life doesn't seem possible. I hear you—I felt the same way. Until I did a fret fast.

You've heard of fasting, of course, where you abstain from something for a specific time to devote yourself to a higher purpose. Abstention is usually from food, but it can be bad habits, too. The Bible contains scores of scriptures about fasting, including Matthew 6:16–18, which comes right after Jesus gives His followers the Lord's Prayer as the example of how to pray. He then launches into instructions for fasting, which is obviously a factor of faith that Jesus encourages (when performed secretly with an attitude of humility, not pride). He concludes with the promise, "And your Father, who sees what is done in secret, will reward you" (Matthew 6:18 NIV).

So if Papa God rewards us for fasting, then it's something we should consider doing, right? But remember, it doesn't always have to be about food.

I've food-fasted at times when my soul was in turmoil about something specific and when I've earnestly desired to petition the Almighty on a deeper level. This time I decided upon a two-week fret fast with the goal of disciplining myself out of the worry habit. To learn not to take the vexations of the world on my shoulders and feel as if I must solve every problem of every person I love every minute of every day. Whew! Before you know it, all that fretting can snowball into:

F: False sense of
R: Responsibility for
E: Every little
T: Thing

I knew a fret fast would be hard because old familiar habits are a bear to break. And it was, most certainly, but sooo worth the effort. Every time I started to fret, I launched into one of the seven anti-worrywart tools listed above and then gradually worked my way through the others as time and circumstances permitted. Some days I'd feel like I was winning the worry battle, and other days, not so much. But by the end of two weeks, I noticed a vast improvement in my emotional outlook.

The freedom of spirit I experienced brought exhilarating joy to my soul and introduced me to a new level of closeness and dependence on my Papa God. That freedom was the soul sister to worship! I felt unbound from worry. . .unconstrained, unrestricted, set loose. Sweet liberation! Ruth Graham said, "Worship and worry cannot exist at the same time in the same heart. They are mutually exclusive."

My conclusion? I don't have to worry. My loving Father really will take care of me if I just let go of my worries and trust Him. Things may not always turn out the way I want, but they'll always turn out the way He wants. And when I'm not weighed down with the faux burden I've placed upon myself to worry things into happening, I have freedom to enjoy the act of living. To live in this moment, not live in the future or relive the past. To enjoy—yes, enjoy—this amazing gift of life I've been given with a big, goofy grin on my face.

Because fretting is not God's best for us. Peace is God's best for us.

So if a two-week experiment changed my life that much, why don't I extend it to a month? Six months? Six years? Well, I'm working on it. Worrywarts take time to dissolve.

> Blessed is the person who is too
> busy to worry in the daytime and
> too sleepy to worry at night.
>
> UNKNOWN

More Pluck, Less Chicken

1. Do you tend to worry more during the daytime or at night?
    What do you worry about most often?

2. Have you found that you worry about different things in
    different seasons of your life? What did you worry about
    this time last year? Did your worrying change anything?

3. Which three of the anti-worrywart tools I've listed seem
    like something you could implement this week?

4. Where is your happy place? Close your eyes, breathe slowly
    in and out, and picture yourself there right now. . . . How
    do you feel?

5. Would you consider a two-week fret fast for yourself? I
    know it seems scary at first, and sort of unrealistic, but
    believe me, it's doable. Now quit harping on all the reasons
    why it won't work and just do it. Grab a girlfriend and do
    a fret fast together—you can encourage each other along
    the way and celebrate together at the end. I promise you it
    will be one of the most worthwhile things you've done for
    yourself this year.

Chapter 7

Look, Sure, but Don't Forget to Leap
(Taking Risks)

*I am about to do something new.
See, I have already begun!*

ISAIAH 43:19 NLT

༄

*M*e? Write a novel? You've gotta be kidding. I haven't written anything deeper than a Christmas newsletter for the past twenty-five years, and you think I should write a whole book?"

Okay, I'll admit my reaction to this new assignment from Papa God nine years ago wasn't exactly awe-inspiring, but I was completely flabbergasted. There, sitting in a dentist office at the ripe age of forty-five, with my youngest chick about to fly the coop, I felt like something was missing. Like there was something I was supposed to be doing. I just didn't have a clue what.

I picked up a magazine and randomly flipped pages. It opened to an ad for a writing contest. Suddenly, a lightbulb flashed on inside my head, and I heard an unmistakable still, small voice speak to my heart, *Deb, it's time.*

Yeah, right. Nuh–uh. No. No, really. . .You don't mean. . .
Gulp.

Seriously?

Well, it's true that I'd harbored a secret childhood dream of being a writer, but life, as it tends to do, took me in an entirely different direction. After twenty-five years, I was still enjoying my career as an orthopedic occupational therapist and was just winding up twenty years as a piano teacher. Raising my two kids had been a wonderful adventure, and I was sad to see it coming to an end. For the past year I'd been getting the niggling feeling that there was more. Something different. Something new.

And the thought made my bejeebies up and run away.

I've never really been the brave type, the daring soul who would leap into anything without a good hard look. And then more often than not, when a situation got the least bit hairy, I'd turn and walk away. By no stretch of the imagination would you call me a risk-taker.

But here I was, standing at the cusp of one of the biggest risks I'd ever faced. Could I do it? Should I even try? What about the heads shaking and eyes rolling, the wasted time and energy, the sheer humiliation if I bombed?

For heaven's sake, Deb. Get a grip, I said to myself. *Are you a wuss or a warrior?*

And then, as if on cue, I remembered the family story about my grandfather, Archie Rogers, a poor farmer in rural Georgia in the 1920s, who had risked everything when he turned down an invitation to join the KKK. In that day and part of the country, you'd best not say no to that particular invitation if you valued your life—it meant you were rejecting the morals and influence of a very persuasive faction of society that didn't take kindly to being offended.

In the Klansmen's eyes, Granddaddy's refusal was like a chaw of tobacco spat on their boots.

We don't know all the details, but I can well imagine what happened next. For months, Granddaddy, a quiet, gentle, unassuming man, went about his business, running the family's small dairy and working as a mechanic, tinkering on tractors and pickup trucks to bring in a little extra money. And most of all, keeping a cautious eye on his wife and four young daughters.

Then several hours before dawn one dark night, a fire mysteriously erupted and in no time consumed their frame farmhouse. Miraculously, my grandparents were able to get all the children out safely before the walls collapsed into ashes. Everything they'd worked and scrimped and sacrificed for. . . gone.

But you know what? They didn't stay homeless. Or distraught. With the help of compassionate neighbors, they rebuilt on that very spot, and the wonderful old farmhouse in which my mother was later born still stands today—a testimonial to resilience when risk-taking gets scary.

Living on the Edge Feels Awfully Sharp

Becoming a risk-taker is, well. . .risky. Probably because most of us prefer our safe little lives of relentless repetition. They're just so ding-dang comfortable. Why change something that's no muss, no fuss, to risk appearing ridiculous, or incompetent, or just plain wrong?

Why chance resurrecting from its shallow grave your carefully buried fear of public humiliation?

I'll tell you why: because God intended our lives to be abundant: "I have come that they may have life, and that they may have it more abundantly" (John 10:10 NKJV). And living abundantly includes facing a series of opportunities that requires taking risks.

We mustn't be afraid to try something new. Helen Keller said, "Life is either a daring adventure or nothing." Cinderella, who had never been to a ball before, was overheard marveling, "One shoe can make all the difference." Noah had never built even a dinghy before he took on the ark.

I heard a story about a gal who worked a repetitive job plucking chickens. All she did hour after hour, day after day, was stand at a conveyor belt, pulling feathers off dead chickens. When asked if she found her job boring, she flashed a big smile and replied, "Of course not! You get a brand-new chicken every thirty seconds."

I wonder how many of us have this plucky chicken-plucker's optimistic attitude about doing the same thing over and over again. It lulls most of us to sleep—just not on the outside where it shows.

There's something about trying new ventures that re-spunks our boredom, revitalizes our weary spirits, and puts a little spring into our flip-flops. Hey, we've gotta go for the sauce in life, not settle for a bland slab of meat.

Daring to do something you've never before attempted awakens your inner child. You remember her—the mischievous, giggly, freckled imp who used to love balancing atop the playground seesaw, launching herself down the slide headfirst, dreaming of riding a unicycle, flying through the air on a rope swing, and enthusiastically trying anything that remotely promised fun.

So where has that adventurous kid gone?

Nowhere. Did you hear that, girlfriend? Nowhere. She's still here. A little jittery, maybe. A bit more cautious and occasionally more emotionally irrational than she used to be. . .because she's peeking out from beneath all those blankets of insecurity you've heaped on top of her all these years. But she's alive and well and it's up to you to reach down, grab her hand, and pull her out so she can remind you about a thing or two you used to know.

Things like doing something outrageous now and then that scares the bejeebies out of you is actually healthy. We were created to thrive from a little excitement. That's why roller coasters and fast cars are so popular. It's those savory thrills that keep us alert, activated, and feeling alive! If you stop doing new things, you'll turn into a tree stump. And sooner or later the termites of atrophy will gnaw away at you until you're nothing but sawdust. Limp, lifeless, useless sawdust.

Now, really, is that the kind of life you want? Absolutely not!

You Have to Get It in Gear before You Can Move Forward

To be a risk-taker, to actually follow through in breaking out of tired old patterns and trying on innovative new adventures, you have to be willing to override your:

- need for approval,
- fear of appearing foolish,
- inflexibility,
- security addiction,
- burning desire to know every possibility,
- fear of pain, and
- drive to be in control.

Sometimes we're stuck in neutral because we're simply creatures of habit. The same ol', same ol' is as unintimidating as an old shoe. It may be scuffed and battered and holey—and not really working very well anymore—but we've finally broken it in and rue going through the process all over again with a new pair. It's just easier to limp along and ignore the possibility that running and leaping and dancing could be within our grasp. . . with just a little effort and possibly some inconvenience.

Or maybe we blame someone else for throwing up roadblocks that keep us stalled and stymied. Wise woman and humorist Karen Scalf Linamen says in her book *Only Nuns Change Habits Overnight*, "Events and people don't hold us back as much as the power we give to those events and people. People don't exercise control over you, you give them control."

That's a subtle difference, but one that we really must embrace. The only people who have the ultimate power to prevent us from making positive changes are ourselves. And the only power our circumstances truly hold over us is the power we allot to them. We make that decision. And circumstances can be altered by even tiny changes that we initiate.

My mother makes the best strawberry cake in the world. I asked for her recipe so I, too, could make the best strawberry cake in the world. But mine didn't turn out like hers. Instead of light, fluffy, and melt-in-your-mouth, mine was flat, dense, and as rubbery as day-old pancakes. A little sleuthing turned up my mistake. I had omitted one small thing when following her recipe—I hadn't beaten the egg whites stiff before folding them into the batter. I had just dumped them in right out of the eggshell. *What's the difference?* I'd reasoned. *They're both egg whites, right?*

Wrong. It seemed like such a little thing, but it made a huge difference in the results.

Sometimes it's the little changes that result in enormous differences in our lives, too. But we'll never know until we woman up and risk making those changes.

We all know people who have risen above difficult

circumstances to succeed. People who seem driven by something we can't see, something that compels them to tweak and keep re-tweaking their actions, plans, and attitudes until they reach their goals. Something that makes them overcome the fear of tipping their comfort-boats and take a risk.

Good examples are Beethoven, Thomas Edison, Abraham Lincoln, Charles Dickens, Lucille Ball, Sam Walton, Garth Brooks, and J. K. Rowling. Look up their stories—they weren't outstanding accomplishers from birth on. No, they're not-especially-gutsy people who sucked up their fears, overcame obstacles, and took risks to change something about their lives.

They ended up touching a lot of other lives as a result.

Are you ready to do that? To open yourself up to change? To weigh the pros and cons of taking action—even though there may be unknown variables—and make the choice to do whatever is necessary to avoid a tree-stump existence?

Let me tell you a hilarious true story about someone who did.

Now You Have Something to Be Thankful For: You're Not Her

$\mathcal{O}$nce upon a time there was a fortysomething gal named Jodi. Jodi had always wanted to ski but had never been brave enough to take the risk. Then one winter, two of Jodi's girlfriends asked her to join them on a four-day, girls-only vacation at a ski resort.

After a little—okay, a lot—of vacillating about whether to go or not, Jodi finally decided she was tired of always spectating life instead of actually living it. She opted to take the plunge and try something new. So she proceeded to dig out her long johns, borrow a pair of waterproof ski pants, and purchase a pair of ski goggles.

When they arrived at the resort, Jodi hit the bunny slopes.

Wow! Skiing was fun! It was stopping that was the bugger.

By the third day, Jodi was feeling so comfortable on the bunny slopes that she promoted herself to the adult green runs. Everything was going great until she suddenly felt nature calling. No, nature was screaming. So Jodi glided over to a clump of bushes bordering the slopes near a stand of trees and looked every which way to make sure she was hidden from view of the skiers schussing by. She braced herself with one ski pole, pulled down her pants, and squatted.

But she'd forgotten to take off her skis. One ski started losing its grip on the icy surface and then the other. Jodi began sliding down the steep hill, unable to alter her course until she ran into a group of unsuspecting skiers talking on the edge of the slope. They fell like bowling pins.

Jodi was so mortified, she hastily gathered up her britches— and her dignity—and quietly slipped away during all the confusion. She decided that disaster was the grand finale to her big skiing adventure.

So the next day, as her girlfriends enjoyed their last hurrah on the slopes, Jodi sipped hot chocolate inside by the lodge's cozy fireplace. There she encountered a man with his leg in a cast. Just to make friendly conversation, Jodi asked, "My goodness, what happened to you?"

"It was the oddest thing," he replied, shaking his head. "I was just standing there talking to my friends yesterday when some half-naked woman tackled me from behind and broke my leg."

Okay, so maybe risk-taking doesn't always pay off.

But that doesn't negate the fact that it often does.

The conclusion to my writing story I started at the beginning of this chapter has a much happier ending. Through much prayer and frequent pleas of "Help-me-Lord-I-know-not-what-I-do," I mustered up the gumption to take the risk and try a new profession. The result was the literary variation of an old nursery rhyme: First came love, then came marriage, then came Debbie with a typewriter carriage. Yep, I met, courted, and then tied the knot with the written word. I've now enjoyed nearly a decade in this committed relationship.

So what about you? What match made in heaven is hovering just outside your view, waiting on you to make the move to discover it?

If at first you don't succeed,
skydiving is not for you.

KAREN SCALF LINAMEN

More Pluck, Less Chicken

1. How about you, girlfriend—are you a wuss or a warrior? A guess-maker or a risk-taker? When was the last time you tried something new?

2. What does John 10:10 mean to you? Would you say you're currently living an abundant life? What are some changes you might need to make toward that end?

3. Have you been in touch with your adventurous inner child lately? What types of insecurity blankets have you piled on top of her over the years?

4. Are you considering possible changes in your life? Which changes make your bejeebies want to up and run away? Why?

5. Are there any circumstances or people that you feel are holding you back from making positive changes in your life? What can you do to change that?

Chapter 8

This Is Only a Test
(Anxiety)

Search me, God, and know my heart;
test me and know my anxious thoughts.

PSALM 139:23 NIV

*D*id you catch the last part of that verse? "Test me and know my anxious thoughts." Is it just me, or do you, too, find the anxiety test awfully hard to pass?

It all starts so innocuously. I awake, as usual, before sunrise, feeling optimistic about the new day yawning promisingly before me. Padding silently across the bedroom carpet, I flip off the alarm clock on my dresser before it has a chance to rudely jerk Spouse from blissful Slumberland. (In truth, I don't even know what my alarm sounds like, because the ridiculously competitive rooster in my head feels he must always crow his fool head off a good hour before whatever time my alarm is set to go off.)

My poodle pal, Fenway, and I take our first walk of the day in the pink, misty light of dawn and all is well with my soul. Or at least all is pleasantly drowsy with my soul, and that's well enough for me at 5:30 a.m.

Back home, after perusing newspaper funnies over a bowl

of granola, I dress, brush my teeth, try in vain to tame the hay sprouting from my scalp, and dutifully swallow my nasty calcium supplement (can you say "melted chalk"?). Tranquility pervades my little world.

Okay, now I'm ready, willing, and as excited as one can be at this hour to start my writing workday.

But something totally weird happens between the brief time I leave the security of my warm, cozy girl cave (kitchen) and slip into the denim computer chair in my office. Suddenly, my inner peace is shattered. Out of nowhere, a weed of inexplicable apprehension takes root in my heart and begins to sprout tendrils that snake around my hapless insides, squeeze my lungs like ripe lemons, slither into my brain to choke all newborn thoughts, and cause my fingers hovering over the keyboard to tremble like a rattler's tail.

Hey, what on earth is happening to me?

The first few times it happened, I had absolutely no idea. Sweat broke out on my forehead and my breathing became funky, shallow and stilted. The pulse in my neck thumped like a bass drum, and I found myself nervously pacing the room, unable to concentrate. It didn't make sense at all. I was a mere rat's whisker from bursting into tears because of. . .what? I didn't have a clue.

Now I know that I was having the first of what I call mini-anxiety attacks (MAAs for short). They're not officially diagnosed as full-blown panic attacks, but they give me a little insight into what those might feel like, and a truckload of sympathy for the tens of thousands of folks who are T-boned by them regularly.

A panic attack is a medical condition defined as the sudden onset of a period of intense apprehension that usually peaks within ten minutes and can linger for an hour or more. No one really knows know what causes them, but they're more widespread than most of us realize.

Symptoms vary but often consist of the same ones I mentioned above regarding my MAAs, but more intense to the point that many think they're having a heart attack and rush to the ER. Additional physical symptoms—which thankfully I've never experienced—can include nausea, numbness, a choking sensation, chest pain, "electric skin," or dizziness. Many folks report an overwhelming feeling that they're dying or having a mental breakdown. Or both.

Scary stuff.

More women than men experience these intense responses of the sympathetic nervous system, and studies show that there may be a higher incidence in people with above-average intelligence. (Small comfort for those who battle them.)

Triggers invoking panic attacks can be internal, like a significant life change or personal loss. Or triggers can be external, such as encountering an object or situation that dredges up a deep-seated fear. For example, thunderstorms elicit panic attacks for one woman I met, because of the fear she experienced when her sister was struck by lightning as a child. One little clap of thunder and she's trembling beneath the nearest bed.

Caffeine, alcohol, and nicotine can also act as triggers for these irrational, over-the-top emotional responses that leave the sufferer reeling.

Real People, Real Panic

My friend Don began having panic attacks after losing 150 pounds in six months (this would be categorized as a significant life change, as mentioned two paragraphs ago). Don's attacks hit him out of nowhere and turned his world upside down.

"Every time I had an attack, I felt like I was going to die. I am not speaking figuratively. . .I mean, I really felt like I was going to die." Don, a successful radio producer, found that lying down helped him relax, ride out gigantic waves of anxiety, and reduce the severity of his symptoms, although at times it weirded-out his coworkers to discover him spread-eagled on the floor of his studio.

Medication and counseling were prescribed by Don's doctors, but he found in the end that "without faith, there is no recovery. Not from anxiety. . .not from anything." Matthew 17:20 became Don's anchor: "I tell you the truth, if you had faith even as small as a mustard seed, you could say to this mountain, 'Move from here to there' and it would move. Nothing would be impossible" (NLT). Don began tucking a packet of mustard seeds into the visor of his truck to remind him of the importance of faith in his recovery. Years later, they're still there. And still just as meaningful.

Don adds, "In the long run, I've become much stronger. As my faith increases, my fear abates. Every time I become afraid, I remember, 'I can do all things through Christ who strengthens me' [Philippians 4:13 NKJV]. I admit that I'm powerless, but I know the One who has all the power. And that makes all the difference."

Fortunately, Don's panic attacks didn't escalate into agoraphobia (fear of open spaces) like many people experience. . . people like Women of Faith veteran Patsy Clairmont. Patsy's account of her downward spiral from avoidance of nerve-rattling situations into self-inflicted emotional and physical imprisonment first in her home, then in her bed, is chronicled in her book *Stained Glass Hearts*.

Patsy, even as a believer, was unable to accept responsibility for running away from people and things that intimidated her.

In her mind, her fear-avoidance behavior was always someone else's fault and out of her control. Patsy downed tranquilizers like candy and became drug dependent.

After suffering hundreds of debilitating panic attacks, Patsy finally reached a breaking point. This was not living. She was the equivalent of a breathing corpse. Something had to change. One morning, while she was hiding beneath her blankets, Patsy heard her Savior's still, small voice whisper three life-changing words to her tormented heart: *Make your bed.*

No kidding.

Although at first "Make your bed" didn't sound much like a divine directive from the Master of the universe, it was brilliant, really. It was so unexpected, it snagged her attention. So simple . . .it was something she could actually do. Patsy felt powerless to address the mountain of problems in her life, but by golly, she could make her bed. And by making her bed, she couldn't still be cowering in it. She had to get up and start putting one shaky foot in front of the other on the long, twisting road back to living.

"I realized that I could begin to get well by choosing different thoughts and different actions," Patsy acknowledges. Through the Holy Spirit's power, she began corralling her reckless emotions and refusing to allow fear to dominate her. "When I gave up coddling my fear, the panic subsided and in time, the symptoms faded."

Don and Patsy are examples of people who at first were overwhelmed by what felt like their own bodies betraying them. They felt out of control, completely at the mercy of the strange, frightening symptoms assaulting them.

I really get that. I bet you do, too.

Don and Patsy, like many other anxiety overcomers, refuse to believe the lie that feelings dictate truth. That because we feel fear gripping our arms, compressing our hearts, and wrapping its tentacles around our windpipes, we have no choice but to allow it to lock us in its smothering embrace. Don't you believe it either. . .feelings do not dictate truth. The reality is that truth should dictate feelings. Fear is not a physical "thing." It can't force you to do anything. Fear only exists in the emotional realm, and you are not a slave to your emotions.

Respect Yourself More Than Your Fear

One of mankind's oldest and strongest emotions is fear. Remember how Adam and Eve fearfully hid from God in the Garden of Eden after they'd sinned? Yep, fear has been around a long time. But we have one very important consolation: The only emotion older and stronger is love. God loved Adam and Eve before and after they'd sinned. Sure, He was disappointed and upset with them because of their disobedience (just like we are when our children disobey us). But He still loved them.

And love—for ourselves as well as our Creator—is a strong motivator to help us conquer our fears.

Whether we battle full-blown panic attacks or lesser, everyday varieties like my MAAs, here are some techniques that have worked for Don, Patsy, myself, and others who were kind enough to share their personal experiences with me.

- Don't panic over panic. Anxiety attacks do not mean that you're mentally ill, so don't fall into the trap of thinking you're losing your mind. Nope, you're not nuts. You're human. Don't ignore them and assume they'll go away, but don't obsess over them either. Increased anxiety over the thought of having an attack can bring one on and you create a vicious cycle. Focus on breaking the cycle.

- Seek help. There's no shame in admitting you can't claw your way out of the anxiety pit alone. Remember, God is the Creator of our best selves, and He's got a terrific you in mind. But you must move your pride out of the way, ask Him to provide the help you need, and take the first step. We can't embrace change until we let go of fear.

- Believe that you have a choice. That's right—believe that you don't have to be controlled by your emotions, even though you might have been bronco-bucked by your berserk feelings for so long, you feel helpless and hopeless about harnessing them. Joshua 24:15 directs us to "choose today whom you will serve" (NLT). Time to decide. Will you choose to serve your crazy, runaway feelings, or the One who created them in their purest form to protect you?

- Identify your insecurity. I believe that insecurity is the bottom line for much of the anxiety we experience. For instance, I've concluded that the basis for those hideous MAAs that shake me to my bone marrow when I'm preparing to write is my underlying fear that it's all a mistake and I really can't write. That I've hoodwinked my publisher so far, but at any moment the truth will become evident and I'll go down in flames. Now I'm not hinting that you should drop an e-mail lovin' on me a little bit (although that would be lovely!), nor do I question my calling from Papa God to this ministry. But that tiny pinch of insecurity yeast—you know, the one right from the Fire and Brimstone Bakery— tends to swell, permeate, and override my rational subconscious thinking processes until all reason is buried. Deep. So deep, I'm not even aware of the real problem. Until I dig. And pray. And consider. How about you, girlfriend? Is bottom-line insecurity causing your anxiety, too?

- Feed your boldness, starve your triggers. You may be surprised that when you boldly step up to fear and grab his beard, his mask comes off in your hands. Surround yourself with people and things that nurture, encourage, and uplift you. Do it for the same reason you work out to de-jiggle your thigh-u-lite. Tone up. Strengthen your emotional muscles for your next confrontation with fear. Identify your triggers and stay far, far away from that which is likely to spark your anxiety and weaken your reserves. Take care of yourself with the same kindness and protection you would give your beloved daughter or son. Children grow and leave, but you're going to be your own BFF for the rest of your life.

- Tap into supernatural strength. Arm yourself with powerful spiritual ammo for the next round before shots ring out. Get out your Bible and focus on at least one of the following scriptures (or any of the verses that speak to you from the beginning of each chapter). At the first sign of anxiety, redirect your thoughts toward these five powerful truths about Papa God and let truth dictate your feelings . . .instead of the other way around:

1. Philippians 4:6–7: He'll give you peace.

2. Psalm 32:7: He'll protect you.

3. Deuteronomy 31:6: He'll go with you anywhere.

4. Psalm 46:1: He is always present.

5. Philippians 4:13: He'll supply the strength you need.

- Remember that as faith increases, fear decreases. Cling to Don's wise discovery: Faith and fear are inversely proportional.

- Set small goals. Patsy's breakthrough was "Make your bed." A simple, tangible directive she could accomplish that started her moving in the right direction—versus being paralyzed into immobility. Small accomplishments pave the way for greater accomplishments.

Do you remember those anxiety tests we talked about back at the beginning of this chapter? Well, girlfriend, there will no doubt be times when we're on the brink of flunking an exam. But you know what? Papa God is more than willing to grade on a curve.

> Courage doesn't always roar.
> Sometimes courage is the little
> voice at the end of the day that
> says "I'll try again tomorrow."
>
> MARY ANNE RADMACHER

More Pluck, Less Chicken

1. What is an anxiety test that you feel that you passed with an A (or at least a B+) in the last six months? What's one that you scored a C- or worse on recently?

2. Do you ever struggle with the lie that feelings dictate truth? In what way?

3. What has been your personal experience with the concept that faith and fear are inversely proportional?

4. Do you agree that insecurity is often the bottom line for anxiety? Can you pinpoint the source of your insecurity?

5. What's your favorite spiritual ammo verse for anxiety?

Chapter 9

Hung Up
(Controlling Obsessions)

*I will not fear though tens of
thousands assail me on every side.*

PSALM 3:6 NIV

$\mathcal{I}$ have to grin when my daily prayer walk takes me by my girlfriend Eddie's house and I see the large ornamental butterfly decorating her front flower bed. Not because the colorful metallic structure poised in flight is beautiful art, although it is. No, I smile because I know a secret about that butterfly. It's a very special butterfly. Its name is Ebenezer.

"Now why would anybody name a lawn ornament?" you might ask.

For the same reason Eddie has a lizard statue in the backyard, also called Ebenezer, and an alarmingly real-looking, three-feet-tall plastic doll standing in her front window. (Eddie calls her Numa, after a doll that came to life in an Alfred Hitchcock show, but I think she should be Numa-nezer.)

You see, these aren't just random decorations Eddie picked up at a trendy boutique; they truly are Ebenezers. Check out this very cool Old Testament story:

> *Samuel begged the LORD to rescue Israel. . . . The LORD*
> *answered his prayer and made thunder crash all around*
> *them. The Philistines panicked and ran away. . . . The*
> *Philistines were so badly beaten that it was quite a while*
> *before they attacked Israel again. After the battle, Samuel*
> *set up a monument. . . . He named it "Help Monument"*
> *[or "Ebenezer"] to remind Israel how much the LORD had*
> *helped them. For as long as Samuel lived, the LORD helped*
> *Israel fight the Philistines.*
>
> 1 SAMUEL 7:9–13 (CEV)

The Ebenezers that surround Eddie are exactly that—Help Monuments, reminders of the oppression she escaped after five decades. A testimonial to God's help in overcoming her many fears.

Eddie was the fifth of seven children raised in a family struggling to get by in Newark's inner city. With little supervision from her always-working parents, Eddie (yep, instead of a boy named Sue, she's a girl named Eddie) was teased and sometimes tormented by her older brothers. One, clutching a butterfly, chased her, threatening, "If I touch you with this, you'll turn into a caterpillar!"

(Yeah, I know—if he was touching it, why wasn't he a caterpillar? But we all recognize that fear isn't always logical, right?)

Another brother sneaked Numa all over the house, making the life-sized doll Eddie had received at Christmas suddenly appear in doorways and closets, as if Numa had walked there on her own. (Incidentally, if you're wondering why Eddie still has Numa forty-five years later, remember the old saying, "Keep your friends close but your enemies closer"? Eddie was always afraid if she gave the nomadic doll away, Numa would come back, and that would be even worse.)

The creepy gift that keeps on creeping.

Speaking of creeping, vermin are an unfortunate fact of inner-city life, and rats were common in Eddie's building. Anxiety was Eddie's constant companion during long dark nights when the snap of rat traps made her envision the filthy rodents crawling up the tassels of her bedspread.

Terrified of the dark, Eddie often stared at her closed bedroom door for endless hours, dreading the moment that doorknob would turn to admit a ghost. These fears were fed by Eddie's mother's rendition of the time she attended a family funeral while she was pregnant with Eddie, and a relative predicted that her baby (Eddie) would be "marked" as someone who could see ghosts and evil spirits.

(A Deb thought here: We adults must beware of our careless words unintentionally planting irrational fears in the minds of children. Kids don't always catch our "Can you believe this nonsense?" overtones, and we may convey something we don't intend. I don't know if Eddie's mother believed this "marked" business or not, but by relating the story repeatedly to her impressionable child, it became true in Eddie's eyes.)

Caution was the norm when everyday life in the inner city included carrying chains for protection and avoiding race riots raging in the littered streets. Break-ins were so common, Eddie learned to sprinkle baby powder on her door stoop when leaving for school in the morning so when she and her siblings returned home in the afternoon, telltale footprints in the powder would warn of intruders.

Eddie and her family finally moved the summer Martin Luther King Jr. was killed and a bullet shattered their front window.

But instead of enjoying the peace of her new suburban home, Eddie had a hard time adjusting. It was too quiet to sleep, with no ambulance noises or shouting in the streets. She found the chirping of unseen outdoor insects scarier than rats in the old apartment.

Since her momma had always warned—for her children's protection—that they'd surely drown in water over their heads, Eddie and her siblings had never learned to swim, so she couldn't bring herself to join the neighborhood kids at the local pool. She was petrified of the water.

Closet Fears

Okay, fast-forward three decades. Eddie, by the grace of God, had finished college, gotten a good job, married a wonderful man named Don, and borne two fine sons.

Try as she might, Eddie had a hard time hiding her fears from her family. Especially the day Don came home with a bouncing boxer puppy for the boys. They were thrilled. Eddie was mortified. In a sudden flashback, she was once again a screaming eight-year-old on top of the parked car in the inner city where she'd clawed her way up to escape a snarling dog that had chased her down the street. She'd been unable to move a muscle until her brother rescued her thirty minutes later. She had been afraid of dogs ever since.

And now, her past had invaded her present.

As an adult, Eddie just couldn't shake her old terrors. She hid in the bathroom until someone removed the puppy from the hallway. She panicked when he jumped up to lick her hand. She avoided him as much as possible and for years did everything standing so he wouldn't leap into her lap or sit beside her on the couch.

And it wasn't only the dog phobia that plagued her. All closet doors had to be opened wide before she went to bed at night (you never knew when Numa—or something even worse—might be hiding in there), and Eddie only bought comforters, never bedspreads with tassels or anything that touched the floor and could serve as a rat ladder. Even though there were no vermin, sometimes she'd be up all night with a flashlight, on the lookout for rats.

After the boys left for college, Don's employer transferred him to Florida. Knowing that all the northern relatives would soon be visiting their new tropical paradise, Don opted for a pool home while Eddie was still up north packing. When Eddie arrived, she was at first aghast over the eight-feet-deep death-hole in her backyard, and then completely paralyzed by the scrub lizards and butterflies everywhere she looked. She immediately envisioned herself tumbling into the pool while escaping from the slithering and flying creatures, dying a flailing, watery death. Her solution was to keep the glass doors to the lanai closed at all times with the blinds drawn. She became a prisoner in her own home.

Poor Eddie saw no way out. "Certain fears run so long and so deep that you don't think about conquering them because you don't realize it's even possible."

It was at this time that Eddie discovered our neighborhood Bible study. Although she was quite reserved at first, she gradually opened up and began to trust the caring group of gals who are her spiritual sisters today. When Eddie finally felt comfortable enough to confide a few of her incapacitating fears, Carolyn from down the street shared with her Joyce Meyer's *The Spirit of Fear* CD set.

Eddie was surprised to learn that she was not alone in her fear battle, that there were, in fact, millions who felt equally discouraged and defeated. Joyce's assertion that the spirit of fear can attach itself to people, often as children, struck a chord with Eddie. And she was energized by Joyce's "Do it afraid" advice. It was the first time in Eddie's life she realized that she didn't have to conquer her fears before she could function like a "normal" person. She could, indeed, do the reverse. First step out in faith to do what she needed to do, depending on God to faithfully diminish her fear in time.

Eddie finally had enough of her self-inflicted imprisonment. After much prayer and spiritual preparation, she was truly ready to confront those fear monsters nose-to-snout. She resolved to do whatever it took to obtain freedom.

Whatever it took. It was commitment time.

Although she'd tried—and failed—adult swimming lessons three different times in the past (she never could put her face in the water), Eddie asked Don to help her learn to swim by baby steps. She was determined to succeed this time. So she purchased goggles and ear and nose plugs. Clinging to Don for support, she began venturing into the backyard pool's shallow end. The goggles enabled her to keep her eyes open (to placate her fear of the dark), and the plugs reassured her that water wouldn't rush in where it didn't belong.

It worked. By the end of the summer, Eddie was able to immerse her head and eventually omit one plug at a time. She finally entered the deep end and learned to doggie-paddle her way to the pool's edge.

Eddie saw this as a huge breakthrough physically, emotionally, and spiritually. At age fifty-four she had finally learned to dance with her first fear monster.

Spurred on by this success (and tons of prayer), she took a course on butterfly gardening and planted bushes that attracted butterflies. Her goal was to desensitize herself by intentionally interacting with the large, colorful monarch butterflies fluttering through her yard every day. Her tongue-in-cheek prayer, as she sat like a stone statue on her garden bench, became, "Lord, if one of these lands on me, at least make me a cute caterpillar."

Before long, Eddie was able to see beauty where before she had perceived only danger. Butterflies, in fact, have become symbolic to Eddie of the joyous freedom from fear she's experienced, and they've become my symbol, too. That's why I asked to have them included on the cover of this book!

People React to Fear but Respond to Love

Irrational fears run amok among us. Did you know that 19.2 million American adults have phobias (extreme fear) about everyday things?[2] Some of the most common phobias include flying, thunderstorms, the dark, specific critters (like snakes, spiders, or dogs), confined spaces, open spaces, tall spaces (heights), and dentists.

Hey, why aren't gynecologists on this list?

Irrational fears are diverse and sometimes hard for the unaffected to comprehend. My fun may be your phobia. Case in point: A hot air balloon ride is high on my bucket list, but floating through the stratosphere in a wicker basket would absolutely kick my height-phobic husband's bucket once and for all. He can't even look out a second-story window without an involuntary shudder and sweat breaking out.

One thing I've learned the hard way: You may not understand the phobias of people you care about, but you must respect them. Don't try to push them into the jaws of whatever they fear until they're ready and willing to deal with the fallout. They can't control their knee-jerk reaction, physical or emotional. If you insist on barraging them with their private fear "for their own good," you (or they) might very well get wounded in the crossfire, and the breach of trust you've created will be difficult to mend.

The good news is that there's definitely hope for overcoming phobias. Many people find professional counseling effective; others have found relief in developing their own coping techniques. Physician-prescribed medication is often helpful. From conversations with Eddie and other gutsy people who are in various stages of overcoming their fear obsessions, I've compiled these tried-and-true tools we can hang on our spiritual tool belts:

- Directly address your fear. That's right—talk to it. Out loud. Rebuke the specific fear and the master deceiver who exploits that fear to control your life. Call it by name. Strip it to its core. Undress that life-sized doll (I'm using Eddie's Numa here to symbolize your personal fear). Grab its plastic body, boldly glare into its glassy eyes, and tell it with God-given authority, "You have no power over me. You're only a _____ [stupid doll; football-sized cockroach; empty closet; man in white with a drill aimed at my teeth . . .specifically name your nemesis]. My fear of you is nothing more than a pathetic ploy of Satan. But I have the Master of the entire universe on my side and He's a lot bigger than you are, punk."

- Become assertive. No more Passive Petunia, you. Resolve to stop meekly accepting Satan's assaulting blows when fear ruthlessly knocks you to the ground with your customized terror. Stand up, girl. Take the first step forward. Even if it's a baby step. It's still a step. Forward. And baby steps add up faster than you think. Next thing you know, you'll be all the way across the room. Remember, fear can only keep you prisoner if you hand over the key.

- Educate yourself. Learn everything you can about the thing that scares you and make lifestyle adaptations based on that knowledge. Take Eddie's lizards, for example. Unfortunately, they're unavoidable in Florida, and we pretty much just have to learn to live with them. (As a native Floridian, I've become lizard tolerant. It's either that or run screaming into the night. Actually, I've been known to clamp a pair onto my earlobes and wear them as funky earrings, but don't tell anybody.) In her research on lizards, Eddie learned that they're repelled by vibration. By playing the praise music channel on the TV placed strategically just inside the doorway (which creates significant vibration against the metal frame), Eddie can now leave the sliding glass door open without guarding it with the broom all day, and simultaneously fill her home with sounds that glorify her Protector. Although she may never feel warm and cuddly toward the teensy gator-wannabes, our girl can now coexist with them.

- Beware of fertilizing your own fear. I call this Boo Poo—manure that feeds the seeds of fear and sprouts stinkin' thinkin'. Mute the power of suggestion. Don't sabotage yourself by watching Indiana Jones battle a pit full of writhing vipers if you're consumed by a snake phobia (or in Eddie's case, don't see Chucky movies if you have a problem with dolls coming to life). Until you're ready—and committed—to desensitize yourself by gradual exposure, censure the fodder you allow into your brain. A haunted brain is far more frightening than a haunted house.

- Practice being unafraid. And be patient. Expect the process of managing your fear to take time. You don't learn to play piano, earn a diploma, or run a marathon in a day. It takes a lot of effort and diligence. Make no mistake, fear management is a learning curve and there may be temporary setbacks. Good days and bad days. In Eddie's case, she practiced muzzling her canine angst by extending one finger every day to touch the vivacious, drooling puppy while Don or the boys held him. After several weeks (and a few unexpected changes of underwear), she added a second finger, and then a third. She celebrated every small victory. Within months she was finally able to place her palm on his back, then eventually his head. Eddie found that through practice and persistence, love trumped fear and she developed a warm relationship with the slobbering source of fright that once curled her hair.

- Ask God to alter your perspective. Eddie's perspective of butterflies changed from that of frightening flying creatures out to harm her, to marvelous creations that bring her joy. What made the difference? Once she was seriously ready to change (and this is the key: seriously ready to change), she proactively planted butterfly bushes to surround herself with the very things that terrified her, and bathed her interactions with them in prayer. Papa God didn't change her eyesight, but He changed her vision.

- Surrender your fear. Analyze the consequences of your fear and its outcome. What's the worst thing that could possibly happen if your worst fears materialized? That you'll die? That you'd close your eyes and wake up in heaven? Is that really a bad thing? In Eddie's words, "I had to give up trying to control things myself because the path to overcoming any fear begins with surrendering it to God. That means being ready in case the very consequence I fear most actually happens, and being okay with it. Because if it does happen, I know it's God's will for me."

- Tap into your competitive spirit. Once you're ready to take that first step forward, do it boldly. Approach conquering your fear as if you're acquiring a brand-new skill. First learn that skill by observing how it's done. Watch those giggling children jump off the diving board into the deep end that gives you shivers. Picture yourself doing it successfully and without qualms. Pretend to be one of the fearless children. Then practice the skill and determine to win; encourage your competitive spirit to kick in. Tell yourself, *If that eight-year-old can do it, I can, too.* Then do it. Stand by that man-eating roller coaster and observe how many people drop dead as they disembark. None? Really? And are they actually smiling? Note to self: "If that lady with the mustache like my great-aunt Matilda can do it, so can I."

- Recognize who is ultimately in control. Is it you? Is it Satan? Is it your worst fear? Or is it the One who created you and wants you to enjoy the marvelous blessings of this bountiful smorgasbord of life experiences set before you? Consider creating a Help Monument to remind you of the answer.

I love the idea of raising an Ebenezer to remind us that God is indeed our power generator. Precious are the modernized lyrics of the glorious old hymn "Come, Thou Fount of Every Blessing," penned in 1758 by Robert Robinson:

Here I raise my Ebenezer; here by Thy great help
    I've come.
And I hope, by Thy good pleasure, safely to arrive
    at home.

Your Ebenezer might not be a butterfly or a lizard or a doll. In fact, your personal monument to God's intervention probably won't mean a thing to anyone else. But it will to you. It will be a symbol that your Father is standing by to help you with every step of your journey home.

There is much in the world
to make us afraid.
There is much more in our faith
to make us unafraid.

FREDERICK W. CROPP

More Pluck, Less Chicken

1. Flip back to the story of Samuel at the beginning of this chapter. Notice the last sentence. After Samuel asked for God's intervention, the Lord helped Samuel fight his battle for as long as he lived. Why would He do any less for you, His daughter, whom He loves more than life itself?

2. What fears do you obsess over?

3. Which fear-fighting tools do you currently employ? Do you think any of those listed in this chapter would be helpful to you? Which ones?

4. Martin Luther said, "I more fear what is within me than what comes from without." What do you think he meant by that? Is it true for you?

5. So what does your Ebenezer (your monument acknowledging Papa God's help in controlling your fear) look like?

Chapter 10

Do They Make Prune Smoothies?
(Uptight about Aging)

Even when I am old and gray,
do not forsake me, my God.

PSALM 71:18 NIV

❧

Fortysomething Josie cracks me up telling the story of the time she got fed up with her thinning eyelashes and paid the friend of a friend—who supposedly was once an aesthetician—to fit her with a beautiful new set of falsies (I'm talking eyelashes, not boobies).

"I only wanted to look pretty," Josie says, shaking her head. "What was I thinking? First, she accidentally glued my eyes shut while applying the eyelashes. Then when she finally got them unstuck, my eyes were flaming red from the adhesive. When the eyelashes hardened, the darn things were so long they kept hitting my glasses so I couldn't blink. They were like these weapons sticking out of my eye sockets. I felt like a Goth drag queen."

Yep, the aging process causes thinning of some body parts and thickening of others. We don't know whether to pad them or pound them. Many of us worry about getting older. According to my fear survey, fear of aging was tied with fear of the unknown/ the what-ifs, and rated a whopping number 2 on the list for those in the sixty-plus age category. Roughly one-fifth of all women surveyed ranked it in their top three fears.

Aging is a peculiar thing. . .just when you begin to grow into your skin, it outgrows you. And the extra has nowhere to go except to hang there all crinkled up like a discarded Twinkie wrapper.

As the evacuation of estrogen makes our upper faces respond with receding hair on our scalps and eyes, our lower faces get even by sprouting dapper little Clark Gable mustaches and random six-inch chin hairs. Hormones also cause (hey, I blame everything on hormones) our derriere rumpage to quadruple, making many of us suddenly feel we are defined by our behind. This additional gel-u-lite forces us to develop drastic new methods of controlling our weight.

Like the ingenious technique author Janette Barber generously shares in *Heavenly Humor for the Dieter's Soul:* "When I buy cookies I eat just four and throw the rest away. But first, I spray them with Raid so I won't dig them out of the garbage later. Be careful, though, because Raid really doesn't taste that bad."

On the subject of cookies and desperation, did you hear about the thirty-one-year-old Naples, Florida, woman who was arrested for chasing her roommate with scissors and whacking her over the head with a board for stealing her Thin Mints?[3] Can you imagine that there are people who would go to jail over Girl Scout cookies? Oreos, I can understand. . . .

Do You Suffer from CDD: Chocolate Deficit Disorder?

*M*y friend Adele says, "When I turned fifty, I turned hungry." I have to agree. In fact, the constant rumbly in my tumbly (was Winnie the Pooh menopausal?) led me to another of the Coty Near-Facts of Science I sprinkle throughout my books. I call this one FAAT: Fabulous Anti-Aging Theory.

FAAT postulates that chocolate actually retards the aging process. I mean, really, what better way to get rid of wrinkles than to fill them out? It's kind of like blowing air into one of the shriveled-up latex examining gloves we use at the rehab center (see how hard I work?)—all the creases disappear and the surface appears as smooth as a baby's bottom. I believe skin works the same way. . .the fluffier it is, the younger it appears. And chocolate is just the stuff to add the fluff. Plus the oils in chocolate act as a terrific moisturizer. . .like the baby's bottom just got lubed with Butt Paste.

So, girls, we're actually helping ourselves by scarfing those M&M's hidden in our ibuprofen bottles!

One-hundred-year-old Peggy Griffith of Abbotsham, UK, would have endorsed my FAAT anti-aging theory. As I shared in my book *Mom NEEDS Chocolate*, this dear little lady claimed that her secret to longevity was consuming thirty chocolate bars per week—per WEEK—since she was ten years old. We're talking fourteen thousand pounds of chocolate in ninety years!

And then there's my writerly friend, Sue Buchanan, author of *I'm Alive and the Doctor's Dead*. Sue is convinced that eating the equivalent of seven chocolate bars every day since she received her cancer diagnosis twenty years ago has been the key to her survival. A world-class choco-athlete like me (that's the step beyond choco-holic), Sue decided to die happy but ended up living happy instead.

Yes, I believe FAAT might have true scientific and sociological merit. . .if not for the downside. Chocolate has calories. Lots and lots of calories. Especially milk chocolate. Sigh. No getting around that unfortunate caveat. With 235 in a typical 1.5-ounce bar, plus additional calories from fillings such as caramel, creams, and nougat, the weight gain from consuming therapeutically large amounts of chocolate could cancel out the health benefits.

Bummer. Mind over platter won't work this time.

On a serious note, weight gain is a legitimate fear for women, ranking in the top 15 on my survey. And closely related is number 10: being judged unfairly.

Of course, judgment is not restricted to weight, but studies show that overweight women often feel judged, even by close friends and family. Notice: They feel judged, whether they actually are or not. That means women may be inflicting the perceived judgment of others on themselves based on their own feelings. In fact, the cultural stigma of obesity is so intense, 15 percent of women surveyed in one study said they'd rather be blind than overweight. Twenty-five percent said they'd rather be severely depressed. Forty-nine percent said they would trade five years of their life not to be obese.[4]

Wow. Does that shock you as much as it does me?

Yet nearly every woman I know is somewhere on the "concerned" to "obsessed" continuum about her weight, so it shouldn't be surprising. I just find it very sad that almost half of us would rather be dead than fat.

The good news is there's something we can do about the fear of weight gain. It's called making good decisions about what we put in our mouths.

Did you know one of the worst culprits for sneaking calories into our diets is drinking them? Health gurus recommend that we intake an average of 64 calories a day by way of sugary beverages, but a twelve-ounce can of regular cola has 140 calories all by its lonesome.[5] That's the equivalent of twelve teaspoons of sugar. Can you imagine eating twelve teaspoons of sugar?

And sweetened tea? Honey, you don't even want to know.

Taking weight off is just the beginning. Keeping it off is a huge challenge. I read about a study that found dieters regain an average of twelve pounds within a year after losing weight. Not primarily from resuming old eating habits, mind you, but because not just one, but six hormones were found to be completely out of whack, causing former dieters to feel persistently hungry.[6]

See—I told you we should blame hormones for everything!

My Gentle Spirit Can Beat Up Yours

Well, it's true many women have a fear of aging and the changes associated with the process. The trouble is that we're constantly aging, from the moment we're born. It never ceases until the day we pack it in, so there will always be someone younger, more energetic, and more attractive than we are.

Comparisons are so unfair. In Galatians 5:26, Paul encourages believers to free themselves from self-judgment: "We will not compare ourselves with each other as if one of us were better and another worse. . . . Each of us is an original" (MSG).

Part of the fear of losing our looks may be because we've always depended on our youthful attractiveness to define our worth. . .to gain admiration from others professionally and personally. To prove that we're competent, smart, or the go-to girl. To project ourselves in a way that solicits respect.

But you know what? While we think it's appearance that draws respect, it's really other qualities like helpfulness, dependability, kindness, and genuine interest in others that truly elevate us in the eyes of others. Sure, appearance does carry a certain amount of influence, but it's inner beauty we should be developing, the evidence of the Holy Spirit's presence in our lives. It's inner beauty that means the most in the end. "You should clothe yourselves. . .with the beauty that comes from within, the unfading beauty of a gentle and quiet spirit, which is so precious to God" (1 Peter 3:4 NLT).

And somehow, inner beauty mysteriously translates into outer beauty. Just look at Corrie ten Boom and Mother Teresa—women whose intangible beauty glowed from within. People who may not have possessed society's standards of physical beauty, but left us basking in the lingering scent of their fragrant inner beauty.

I love what author Sarah Biggs-Wudel wrote about beauty: "What if, as we grow older, the layers we use to coat our minds and souls were like the layers of nacre an oyster lays? How beautiful we would become in old age, like a pearl."

"Like a pearl." Isn't that what we truly want to become? A priceless pearl whose value is determined by layer after layer of unfading beauty born of the friction we've endured throughout our lifetimes?

The key, I think, to assuaging anxiety about aging is to focus more on what we have left than on what we've lost. Gracefully embracing changes that the aging process thrusts upon us is what will keep us active and growing, and vitality is what will keep us attractive.

But occasionally graceful just doesn't work. There are times when rather than embracing, we have to wrestle some of those hard-to-swallow changes into a chokehold by being clever, coy, and creative.

My aging motto is if you can't fix it, decorate it. I learned this important life principle from a broken-down mailbox in my neighborhood. A careless driver backed into it one fateful day and knocked the entire stucco mailbox stand over, breaking it into big ugly chunks and severely denting the metal mailbox. For weeks the stand and box lay there, crumbling and pitiful—an eyesore for the entire cul-de-sac.

Then one crisp October day as I power-walked by, that

very same mailbox brought a smile to my lips. Someone had decorated the pile of debris with wreaths of white-thread spiderwebs complete with adorable little fake spiders (can spiders ever really be adorable?). It was the perfect Addams Family touch for the mailbox whose dings were now camouflaged by sprigs of cheerful fall flowers. That decrepit mailbox took on a whole new cheerful, uplifting personality.

So, girls, it's perfectly okay to pull out our funky red hats, bright colors, and bling jewelry. The wilder, the better! Shiny is delightful. Chunkage is totally acceptable. What works for broken-down mailboxes works even better for broken-down bodies. Feel free to make my aging motto your own: If you can't fix it, decorate it.

The Sky Is Falling!

*O*kay, I don't want to alarm you, but something crazy is going on with our solar system. Have you noticed that earth's gravity is intensifying every single year? Really, it is. You recognize it most when you're undressing for bed. My theory is that the magnetic core of the earth is sucking everything loose toward it like one of those vacuum tubes at the dentist's office that, when you close your lips around it, pops your eyeballs out of their sockets and would suck down your tongue if it wasn't attached back there by your hangy-ball.

I don't know why this Increasing Gravity Phenomenon hasn't made the news. The evidence is right there on the back of my arms and hanging off my chin. Speaking of loose neck skin, if you ask me, the reason so many of us mature, sweetly ripened women develop kyphosis (hunchback) is because we're subconsciously trying to hide the majority of our chins by rounding our shoulders and protruding our heads forward.

I call it the Chicken-Neck Maneuver. (Works pretty well for disguising jowls and wattles, too.)

This gravity thing is doing a nasty number on Freddie and Flopsie, my Bobbing Twins, who've hung around faithfully for decades. The Twins suddenly decided to take an extended vacation in the South of Pants. And I'm not just talking high waters here. I declare, if my little ponies weren't harnessed and corralled, I'd trip over them.

And then there's the Obstinate Orca Propagation Site (OOPS) to contend with. You know—those humpback whales growing on the outside of your upper thighs right where they attach to your hips. Suddenly one morning you wake up and OOPS, there they are, beached orcas, refusing to return to the open sea. My obstinate orcas are named Shamu and Shazam. It's good to be on a first-name basis with your appendages if you're going to do life together. I feed them M&M's instead of plankton.

Sigh. Perhaps the best defense against gravity is levity.

No matter how we look at aging, we really need to count our blessings. It could be far worse. You could be a female kangaroo, pregnant for her entire adult life. The poor gal has to hop till she drops with an embryo in her womb and a joey in her pouch, attached to her nipple. And Jo-Jo stays right there, latched on tighter than a tick, until the little dickens gets old enough to leave home. When he finally goes off to college, the previous embryo promotes herself into the pouch and a new embryo fills her vacated spot in the womb. And the beat goes on.

Perpetual pregnancy. . .can you imagine breast engorgement lasting forty years? Or a hungry little head popping out of your fanny pack to whine every single time you try to sneak a Dove bar? Or sizzling through a hot flash with two extra hot little bodies on board?

Nope, old age ain't for wimps. My friend Ronni says, "If you get through menopause with your husband and one friend left, you're successful!"

When we lose twenty pounds. . .we may be losing the twenty best pounds we have! We may be losing the pounds that contain our genius, our humanity, our love and honesty.

WOODY ALLEN

More Pluck, Less Chicken

1. What was your biggest ever fashion faux pas?

2. Which symptom of aging is currently your biggest nemesis?

3. Robert Schuller said, "A year from now, you may wish you had started today." What does that mean to you in regard to things you want to accomplish before you grow old?

4. What message do you think your appearance projects to the world about your personality? Which qualities do you think you'd like to project even more? How can you make that happen?

5. Romans 12:2 tells us, "Don't become so well-adjusted to your culture that you fit into it without even thinking. Instead, fix your attention on God. You'll be changed from the inside out" (MSG). How can you apply this scripture to yourself?

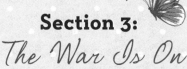

Section 3:
The War Is On

Protecting Ourselves
with the Armor of God

❧

Let the mighty strength of
the Lord make you strong.
Put on all the armor that God
gives, so you can defend yourself
against the devil's tricks.

EPHESIANS 6:10–11 CEV

*I*t's a war out there. And the only way to successfully combat fear is to be prepared for its next attack. Wearing the proper armor is crucial for victory against Satan, Enemy Number One, the mastermind of our worst fears. Each and every item in our spiritual wardrobe is important. For this section, I've focused on one essential component of each of the six pieces that make up the armor of God as described in Ephesians 6:13–18:

- Underwear of Truth: Gratitude
- Breastplate of Righteousness: Compassion
- Boots of Peace: Forgiveness
- Shield of Faith: Perseverance
- Helmet of Salvation: Grace
- The Sword of the Spirit: God's Word

I hope this modern-day slant on eternal truths will help you shimmy into your designer armor. Start styling, girl!

Chapter 11

Chain Mail: The New Silk
(Underwear of Truth: Gratitude)

You shall know the truth,
and the truth shall make you free.

JOHN 8:32 NKJV

𝒜s Thanksgiving approached, the only thing my friend Debbie, mother of eight, found in her freezer was a pound of ground meat. Finances were tight. Her husband had been holding down three part-time jobs since being laid off the year before.

With company coming for Thanksgiving dinner, Debbie really wanted to serve a traditional turkey, so she visited a large metropolitan ministry to which she had donated when times were better. They offered free turkeys for needy families. The conversation there went something like this:

Counselor: "Yes, ma'am, we'd be happy to help you with a turkey if you'll just sign the application. We'll need your food stamp information."

Debbie: "Oh, we don't get food stamps. My husband and I believe that the Lord will supply our needs. We've been blessed with help from caring Christians when we needed it most."

Counselor: "Did you say you don't get food stamps? Step right over to that desk and we'll sign you up for the program."

Debbie: "Um, no sir, we don't want food stamps. We don't believe it's the government's responsibility to feed us."

Counselor: "Well, that's what they're here for. It's the only way you can get a free turkey from us. No food stamps, no turkey."

Debbie left the building empty-handed, wiping away tears and whispering this prayer: "Lord, if it would please You, give us a turkey. We're willing to feast on vegetable soup if that's Your provision, and we'll be grateful. But I want to invite others to join us, and I don't feel comfortable asking them to eat soup for Thanksgiving."

Debbie didn't want to burden her friends or family, so she told no one about this pressing need and left it entirely in the Lord's hands.

Two days later, Debbie's father-in-law, with no knowledge of their plight, dropped by with a large turkey he'd run across on sale. A few days later, someone brought another turkey. Then another. In Debbie's words, "For ten days, the floodgates of heaven opened and packed our freezer with fourteen turkeys, twenty chickens, and forty pounds of venison." Then a grocery store gift card arrived, which provided all the fixings for a bountiful Thanksgiving dinner.

Debbie needed one bird and the Lord provided thirty-four. Plus a herd of deer. Wow! What a God we serve. And what an example of gratitude Debbie is. She was ready to accept— with heartfelt thanks—a pot of soup, but instead she received in-the-flesh verification of Ephesians 3:20–21: "To Him who is able to do *exceeding abundantly above* all that we ask or think, according to the power that works in us, to Him be glory. . . forever and ever. Amen" (NKJV, emphases mine).

Expressing Gratitude

*O*ne of the major truths in God's Word is that He is our Provider. In fact, one of His Hebrew names depicts just that: Jehovah-Jireh (translates "Our Provider" or "The Lord Sees"). He sees our needs and provides for them. There's no doubt of the Source of the blessings we enjoy: "Every good and perfect gift is from above" (James 1:17 NIV).

And how are we to respond when He graciously plops a good and perfect gift in our lap? These are just a few of the verses that address that question—look them up and jot down your answers:

- Psalm 95:2

- Colossians 2:7

- Psalm 69:30

- Hebrews 12:28

- Psalm 147:7

- Colossians 4:2

- Jonah 2:9

- Colossians 3:15–16

Do you see a pattern here? I don't believe Papa God meant for us to thank only Him for the blessings that enrich our lives, but also to thank the people responsible for the little things that make our earth sojourn more pleasant.

Sometimes an expression of gratitude can make all the difference in the world to people who desperately need to know that they count, that we value them. That their actions, however small, are appreciated. . .a harried waitress, the overworked clerk trying to whittle down a long waiting line, a lonely parking lot attendant, the day-care worker up to her elbows in dirty diapers.

In his book *A Simple Act of Gratitude,* Superior Court Judge John Kralik shares his experience in writing nearly a thousand thank-you notes to chronically overlooked people just like these since 2008. In December 2007 he'd hit rock bottom financially, emotionally, and physically. He decided to get his mind off his multitude of problems and focus instead on acknowledging how much other people blessed his life by seemingly tiny, inconsequential kindnesses.

He underestimated the motivational potential of a little appreciation.

John was astounded by the ripple effect of gratitude—those he thanked were suddenly motivated to thank the "little people" in their lives, who in turn felt compelled to thank those in their own lives. Observing the wide-reaching consequences of a simple thank-you, John concluded, "I keep learning that gratitude is a path to the peace we all seek."

Gratitude is an emotion that multiplies itself. That concept is actually supported by science. University of Miami psychology professor Michael McCullough says, "When you are stopping and counting your blessings, you are sort of hijacking your emotional system." You're literally changing your emotional worldview and altering your thinking patterns. Dr. McCullough equates the emotional high you receive from giving thanks to the rush of winning, of experiencing victory. And truly, what could be more victorious than sprouting wings and flying right out of the self-pity muck that so often bogs us down?

Scientists, who in the past have generally disregarded the role of thankfulness, have now discovered that gratitude is one of the most powerful human emotions and can literally make people live longer, happier lives. In fact, gratitude journals are becoming a regular therapy tool used by many psychologists to help their clients reduce fearfulness, connect to others, and improve their emotional outlooks.

The idea is to recognize the people you're thankful for, consider what your life would be like without the things you enjoy, and be intentionally grateful for them. Then take it a step further and express your gratitude. The purpose is to morph your behavior from complaining to thankfulness, and a positive attitude adjustment will follow.

Isn't it terrific that psychology is finally catching on to what the Bible has told us for centuries?

Beautitude: Developing a Beautiful Attitude

Gratitude provides the firm foundation for a strong, resilient, beautiful attitude. Sort of like Spanx, the twenty-first-century girdle. So how do we break out of our longtime habits of grousing and complaining and wriggle into our Thanks-Spanx? How can we drag our weary eyes off ourselves and our urgent unmet needs in order to focus on becoming more thankful? Here are a few suggestions:

- Chart Papa's track record. Jot down your caring Father's intervention in times past—those crucial turning points when He proved His love for you by doing something exceedingly abundantly above (recognize Ephesians 3:20

from Debbie's story?) what you expected. Now parlay that hindsight into foresight and trust Him to take care of you in the future. Thank Him for it ahead of time.

- Focus on the problem-solver, not the problem. Or the next potential problem, or the one after that. Dreading future difficulties that haven't yet materialized is fear sinking its sharp talons into your inner peace. Dwelling on our problems is like staring day after day at the burned muffins, flopped quiche, and rock-hard chocolate-chunk cookies lining your counter rather than picking up the phone and calling the oven repairman. Addressing the source is the key, not lamenting about the symptoms. Call on the life Repairman and tell Him not only your needs, but what you appreciate about His handiwork. Praise Papa God for His caring attributes—patience, forgiveness, faithfulness, grace, healing, protection, provision, renewal, rest, security, and wisdom, to name a few—that are full of loving-kindness for His beloved children. He's always willing to make a house call.

- Relinquish command. Even if some of your questions remain unanswered. Accept the fact that you will most likely leave this earth still not understanding everything. Sometimes we just have to yield to the One who is large and in charge. It's called faith. "Faith is confidence in what we hope for and assurance about what we do not see" (Hebrews 11:1 NIV).

- Reach for the air freshener. Gratitude is Glade for the soul. It revitalizes inner staleness, replaces remnants of decay with fresh flowers, and perks up the living room of our heart. Spray liberally.

- Renew your perspective. Gratitude has a way of opening our eyes to things we wouldn't ordinarily notice—important but often overlooked things that give us a startlingly different perspective. I love the quote attributed to Abraham Lincoln: "I felt sorry for myself because I had no shoes until I met a man who had no feet."

- Hold tightly to thankfulness. When the hard times come—and they inevitably will—gratitude is one of the first things we lose our grip on. So grip harder. Counting our blessings in the midst of trouble is difficult, to be sure, but it's the very thing that will unknot our guts, calm our anguished hearts, lower our defenses, and melt our anger. We *need* to be grateful. . .not just spiritually, but emotionally and physically, too.

- Pray and trust the results. Whatever they are. "Tell God your needs, and don't forget to thank him for his answers" (Philippians 4:6 TLB). Okay, I know that sometimes we don't feel thankful for His answers, especially when troubles fill us with fear, anger, or resentment. Who could feel grateful for a daughter's brain tumor, a foreclosure notice, or a deteriorating marriage? But Papa God didn't specify that we should be thankful only for the good answers—the miraculous healing, winning the lottery, a sudden rekindling of first love—the answers that make our life easier, happier, and stress-free. No, He said to thank Him for all His answers, even when it's "No, My beloved child," "Wait on My perfect timing," or "I'm sorry that you must go through this fire, precious one, but I will go through it with you." We don't have to feel happy about tough circumstances, but if we view the fire-treading moments when we're thankful-by-will-only as an act of faith, believing that our all-powerful, all-knowing Papa God is using even the grinding process of the tough times to sharpen our trust, it will bring us closer to Him. And hey, isn't that our goal?

- Choose contentment. Intentional choices, if practiced enough, become habits. Emulate the most thankful person you know. If no one comes to mind, you need a new crowd, girlfriend. Go out and meet someone whose countenance is joyful and whose eyes twinkle. Make no mistake—friends who do nothing but complain and gripe will drag you down. If you stand beneath a dripping faucet, you will get wet. You need to hang out with upbeat, positive people. In the meantime, fake it until it's real. You won't believe how fast purposely thinking and talking like you have a grateful spirit will actually produce one.

Joyful Transformation

*N*eed an example for that last point? Here's one that will make you smile.

My friend Larissa was raised by quiet, serious parents with very little joy or humor ever exhibited in their home. Larissa consequently became a quiet, serious woman who married a quiet, serious man and raised two quiet, serious children in a quiet, serious Christian home.

Sounds awfully, um. . .quiet and serious, doesn't it?

But Larissa felt something was missing. Around the time her kids left for college, she became convicted that she needed more Jesus-joy, lightness, and humor in her life. Larissa began praying for God to send friends her way who would rub some holy effervescence off on her.

So she fell and broke her wrist (be careful what you pray for). Enter moi, the friendly neighborhood therapist. But I didn't know about her quandary until months afterward, when Larissa and I hosted an old-fashioned tea party for my rehab patients, complete with lace doilies, yummy scones, flowerpot hats, and wild-and-crazy party dresses. We even decorated their wheelchairs and walkers. It was a total blast with lots of zaniness and fun.

It was then that Larissa spilled the beans about reinventing herself and how at first she knew no other way to become joyful than to act joyful even though she didn't feel it. Lo and behold, to her great surprise, it wasn't long before laughter and lightness and Jesus-joy actually flooded her soul and she didn't have to pretend anymore. The Maker of Heaven and Mirth had truly transformed her.

But Papa God doesn't always dramatically alter us the way He did Larissa. Sometimes we just have to find gratitude playing the cards we're dealt. Like Debbie with her pot of soup, and John, who had nowhere to go but up. And the woman I met at a writers' conference who admitted, "I always wanted to be a writer, but I ended up a mortician's wife. I'm actually thankful. I'm going to write a book called *101 Creative Uses for Duct Tape in a Funeral Home.*"

Now that's gratitude for ya!

God gave you a gift of 86,400 seconds today. Have you used one to say "Thank You"?

WILLIAM A. WARD

More Pluck, Less Chicken

1. Name an example of Papa God doing something exceedingly abundantly above all that you ask or think in your life.

2. Name three "little people" whom you can thank to begin the ripple effect of gratitude. Will you commit to jotting them a brief note this week?

3. Elisabeth Elliot said, "It is always possible to be thankful for what is given rather than resentful over what is withheld. One attitude or the other becomes a way of life." How has gratitude altered your thinking patterns and renewed your perspective?

4. Is it difficult for you to implement Philippians 4:6 in the hard times? Why do you think this verse is important for us to take to heart?

5. They say if you sleep with dogs, you're gonna get fleas. Is there a complainer in your life who is sucking away your gratitude? What can you use as flea shampoo?

Chapter 12

Steel Camisole
(Breastplate of Righteousness: Compassion)

As God's chosen people, holy and dearly loved,
clothe yourselves with compassion, kindness,
humility, gentleness and patience.

COLOSSIANS 3:12 NIV

〜

I love the story of the day New York Mayor Florello
LaGuardia officiated in municipal court during the 1940s.
During his three terms as mayor, LaGuardia was the original
"Undercover Boss" and wore the hats of various professions
around the city in order to stay in touch with the needs of the
people.

As the story goes, during LaGuardia's stint as judge, a
little old lady who had stolen a loaf of bread for her starving
grandchildren was brought into court. The fine was either ten
dollars (a considerable sum in those post-Depression days) or
ten days in jail. Surmising the woman's destitute situation, Mayor
LaGuardia reached into his pocket and paid the fine himself, and
then passed a hat around, stating, "I'm fining everyone in this
courtroom fifty cents for living in a city where a person has to
steal bread in order to eat."

The old woman went home with $47.50 in her purse and

hope shining in her eyes.

Mayor LaGuardia demonstrated compassion at its finest in that courtroom.

Compassion is empathetic willingness to enter someone else's distress. To not only share their suffering, but take it one step further in attempting to alleviate it.

In the New International Version alone, I've counted 105 verses in the Bible extolling Papa God's great compassion toward us and urging us to extend compassion toward each other. Whoa. Does that hit you as hard as it hits me? That the Master Designer of all that exists is ready and willing to enter our distress? Our every distress. That He's offering to not only share our suffering, but work diligently to alleviate it?

All because He cares so deeply about you and about me.

And He earnestly wants us to show compassion toward others, too. . .to enter into their distress right alongside them and do what we can to alleviate it. But sometimes we get distracted from this noble mission and focus on alleviating our own distress instead.

I read about a study[7] where rats were put into a testing cage two at a time. One was entrapped in a narrow clear plastic tube so that its squirming discomfort was evident to the other rat, which remained free. A stash of chocolate was then introduced on the other side of the cage as a distraction. (Hey, I'm no rodent, but I can guarantee chocolate would distract me!)

Of the testing group, all six females ignored the chocolate and worked hard to free their partners by pushing in the door to the entrapment tube. They then enjoyed the chocolate together. (Go, girls!)

Although some of the males were first wooed by the chocolate chips and even unpacked them from the container, seventeen of the twenty-four males chose not to eat until they had emancipated their buddies so they could feast together. The other seven turned their furry backs on their distressed partners and wolfed down the goodies all by themselves. One can only hope the selfish seven didn't press their whiskered faces against the tube imprisoning the poor hungry twitching dude while they smugly belched, licked their paws, and scratched their little rat tushies.

The conclusion of the study?

1. Even rats demonstrate compassion.
2. Females show more consistent empathy than males.
3. If rats can be so caring, maybe there's hope for humans.

That last one was offered in jest by the head researcher, but still, it's got merit, don't you think?

In our defense, many humans do demonstrate compassion . . .directly, as in serving at a soup kitchen, raking an elderly neighbor's yard, or visiting a shut-in. We also show compassion indirectly by donating time, energy, and funds to those needing help, for instance, sponsoring a child through such organizations as Compassion International.

My family has sponsored CI children for over twenty years and we've found it immensely gratifying. For roughly one dollar a day, we've been able to make a difference in the lives of children (and their families) who have so little.

I will always treasure their letters, like the one several years ago from our Kenyan child, Alfred, who thanked us profusely for the "she goat," clothing, and maize purchased for his family with the fourteen dollars we sent for Christmas (monetary gifts are limited, but a little goes a long way in impoverished countries). The "she goat" provided milk for Alfred's family and was a valuable source of ongoing income for years to come. This was especially important because Alfred's family consisted of poor farmers who lived in a hut with a dirt floor. Alfred and his brothers never would have been able to complete school if not for Compassion International sponsorships.

The compassion of someone across the world changed Alfred's life. To borrow a surfer phrase, that's righteous, sister! I believe compassion is the steel that makes the breastplate of righteousness impenetrable.

Put Your Breast on a Plate

We've all seen pictures of olden warriors wearing their armor and can surely dredge up a mental image of a breastplate (you can exhale now—this kind of breastplate has nothing to do with mammography).

Even better, picture the breastplate Heath Ledger wore for jousting in the 2001 film *A Knight's Tale* (if you haven't seen the movie, it's a fun blend of ancient and modern woven into a fairy-tale love story). Heath's breastplate had to be strong enough to withstand the impact of a lance thrust by an opponent mounted on a horse galloping toward him at full speed. The thing was designed to protect the vital organs without limiting mobility. Without a breastplate, an enemy attack would doubtless be fatal.

Even with the armor, serious injuries could occur if the sharp tip of the attacking sword, spear, or lance somehow slipped through the armhole or between the breastplate and helmet (as Heath demonstrated in the scary scene where the bad guy cheated by replacing the harmless lance tip with a real spearhead).

Breastplates were important in those days if you wanted to stay alive.

Wonder if they had a girl version. I mean, really, what better way for a woman to protect her heart than to wear a steel bra?

Or a metal camisole? But then she would have had to carry Windex around in her forty-pound iron purse to shine the thing up after dragon blood dripped all over it.

Did you know breastplates were also worn by high priests in Bible days to figuratively protect themselves from unrighteousness? Righteousness means doing right in God's eyes; those priestly guys were symbolically fending off the attacks of the Enemy (Satan), which could very well result in sin and spiritual death.

Then—and now—wearing armor is a precaution to protect yourself from a wily, unscrupulous enemy. We may not use literal steel breastplates today, but we certainly need protection just as strong. You and I are still being attacked daily, although neither our enemy nor our armor is visible to the naked eye. "We are not fighting against humans. We are fighting against forces and authorities and against rulers of darkness and powers in the spiritual world" (Ephesians 6:12 cev).

Angels in Drag

Compassion is one of the primary components of the breastplate of righteousness. In other words, compassion is a symbol of our faith and desire to do what's right in the eyes of God—a vital part of the armor that not only protects us, but marks us as His by our generous outreach to others. And hey, you never know when you might be showing kindness to an angel in disguise. "Do not neglect to show hospitality to strangers, for by this some have entertained angels without knowing it" (Hebrews 13:2 nasb).

Acts of compassion are bright, shiny evidence to the world that we gratefully acknowledge the compassion our Papa has shown toward us, and are likewise willing to enter someone else's distress.

An excellent example is the compassion shown by my friend Rebecca. This is such an awesome story, it give me goose bumps telling it.

Four years after Rebecca chose life for her baby after becoming pregnant at age twenty, Rebecca's coworker Staci, also twenty, found herself in the same frightening position. But she couldn't decide what to do.

Staci's fiancé was not at all supportive, and his parents went ballistic when they heard the news. Besides trying to convince their son the baby wasn't his, they said horrible things about Staci and insisted she take money for an abortion, although she was nearing the end of her first trimester and already knew the baby was a boy.

Staci's world crashed. She saw no choice when faced with the prospect of bringing a child into a world where his grandparents didn't want him and his father doubted he was really his. Staci's heart grew cold and hard. The fetus morphed from "the baby" to "it" in Staci's conversations with Rebecca.

Staci's mind was made up. She would terminate this pregnancy.

Rebecca made no secret of where she stood on the issue (she has footprints of a fifteen-week-old baby tattooed on her foot beside the word PROLIFE). She described the gruesome abortion procedure and even showed Staci video footage of Rebecca's own eleven-week-old son waving his arms and flipping around in utero. But moved by her conviction that true compassion means loving and caring without boundaries, Rebecca assured Staci that she wouldn't judge her; that she would be there for her, not just before, but after as well, no matter what her decision.

The night before the scheduled abortion on Friday at 2:00 p.m., Rebecca couldn't sleep. Her stomach and her mind were churning. So she prayed, "Lord, what more can I possibly do to save this child?"

The local university's Pro-Life Alliance (PLA) president popped into her head, and she remembered that the group gathered outside the abortion clinic each Friday to pray. So she grabbed the phone to ask if the PLA members could watch for Staci the following afternoon. She knew Staci wouldn't stop to talk to them, but she hoped that someone could somehow communicate something indirectly to her that would make a difference.

Rebecca was disappointed to learn that—ironically—the PLA members had plans to man a booth at a campus rally that Friday in honor of Pro-Life Week. No one would be at the clinic at the time of Staci's appointment.

Friday morning finally arrived. Rebecca prayed for a miracle.

Shortly before noon, Rebecca got an e-mail at work from the PLA president saying they'd had a change of heart and all fifteen of them were on their way to the clinic.

At 1:45, Rebecca stretched out a shaking hand for her office phone to call Staci one last time when the cell phone in her purse rang. It was Staci, sobbing. She'd been sitting alone in her car in front of the abortion clinic, watching all these people she didn't know standing around peacefully praying, when she suddenly realized that "it" was a child. The truth sank in. She couldn't kill her baby. She wouldn't kill her baby. She drove home.

Compassion for both Staci and that precious unborn infant drove Rebecca to keep praying and keep trying to find a way even when it seemed impossible. The compassion of fifteen people who cared enough to devote their time and energy to pray for someone—make that two someones—they didn't know made all the difference in that little boy's world. All the difference.

The same way a "she goat" made all the difference in Alfred's world. And Mayor LaGuardia's hat full of coins made all the difference in a penniless grandma's world.

So tell me. . .in whose world can your compassion make all the difference?

*If you haven't any charity in your heart,
you have the worst kind of heart trouble.*

BOB HOPE

More Pluck, Less Chicken

1. How would you rate yourself on a 1 (low) to 10 (high) scale of compassion? Is this a score you'd like to improve?

2. Do you find it difficult to enter into someone else's distress when your own distress is screaming for attention?

3. Can you name a time when you were able to show compassion toward someone else? How did it make you feel?

4. Reread Hebrews 13:2. Have you ever met an angel in disguise? Or at least someone you suspected was an angel? It's kind of cool to think they're out there, isn't it? How does this verse affect your view of compassion?

5. What about Rebecca's story resonated with you? How did you answer the last question of the chapter: In whose world can your compassion make all the difference?

Chapter 13

Is There a Cure for People Hangovers?
(Boots of Peace: Forgiveness)

*You will keep in perfect peace all who trust in you,
all whose thoughts are fixed on you!*

ISAIAH 26:3 NLT

The Hand Conference is crowded this year. I inch through the door, late as usual (spouse says I'm a charter member of the Church of the Better Late Than Never). Glancing around for a seat, I see there are few available in the hotel banquet room where hand therapists and orthopedic surgeons from all over the state have gathered to learn new procedures and catch up with old friends.

I smile to myself as I scan familiar faces that have grown dear over the three decades I've been in this profession. But suddenly, I spot the back of a head I wish I didn't know. The oxygen seems to suck right out of the room.

Oh no! *She's* here. I was sure hoping *she* wouldn't make it this year.

She is Karen, the therapist I had a. . .well, a falling-out with nine months ago. (Falling-out sounds holier than venomous spat, don't you think?) We'd had a history as coworkers and friendly acquaintances for twenty years up to that point, but it all flushed right down the toilet when I cut back my clinic hours (to write my books) and Karen was promoted to supervisor. My boss.

And believe me, she took bossy to a whole new level.

It didn't take long before I began seeing a different side of Karen—the hard-nosed, must-do-it-my-way, snarky personality that had stayed submerged when we were merely peers. My feelings were sorely trampled by a series of inconsiderate actions on Karen's part, and I felt completely justified in cutting off all communication with her when I left that position for a new job elsewhere.

Not unlike a mad kid on the playground, grabbing her toys and running home.

This conference is the first time Karen and I have been under the same roof after all this time. I choose a seat on the opposite side of the room, making sure not to look in her direction.

During the first break, I chat with an old friend who casually mentions, "So. . .are you speaking to Karen yet?"

I swallow. Hard. I didn't realize anyone else knew about our little kerfuffle. I know I haven't told anyone, so it must be coming from Karen. Great. Now she's talking about me behind my back after impaling it with her bloody dagger.

But hey, I'm not bitter. (Cough, hack.)

When I head for the ladies' room, of all rotten luck (or could it be something else?), who should be walking toward me down the narrow corridor? It's her. But when Karen glimpses me approaching, she begins rummaging in her purse and I check my watch for the time, so we cleverly avoid making eye contact.

Unhappy and restless, I return to my seat. Ignoring this problem isn't making it go away. It's just looming there overhead like a dark cloud pregnant with hailstones.

Later that night in my hotel bed, I can't sleep. Something is twitching in my soul and I do not want to admit this spasm of conscience is my fault. I argue with Papa God about the utter injustice of the situation. I remind Him that I'm the one who was wronged here. I'm the victim! Why should I have to be the one to gather the lumber, hammer, and nails to build a bridge?

I finally stop fussing long enough to catch my breath. A still, small voice whispers to my heart, *I know, My child. I know. But the Carpenter will give you all the tools you need. Bridges are His specialty.*

Still muttering about injustice, I grab my Bible on the nightstand and randomly flip the Word open. The jeans on my attitude are suddenly giving me a wedgie and I feel the need to unzip.

The pages fall open to Luke 23, where I read verses 32 and 33:

Two other men, both criminals, were also led out with him [Jesus] to be executed. When they came to the place called the Skull, they crucified him there, along with the criminals—one on his right, the other on his left. Jesus said, "Father, forgive them, for they do not know what they are doing." (NIV)

I lay the Bible down.

A ton of bricks lands squarely on my prideful heart.

Jesus Christ, the only truly innocent person who ever lived, was faced with the ultimate injustice: He was executed in a horrible, excruciatingly painful public debacle for something He didn't do. And He didn't fight it. He didn't scream and rant and rave about the unfairness of it all. He didn't even refuse to look at His offenders.

No. He looked at them all right—He looked right through them and saw raw, wounded, fallible humanity deep beneath the surface of their hateful actions. He compassionately asked God to forgive them because they didn't fully understand the grave atrocity they'd committed. And in doing so, Jesus forgave them, too.

Isn't my goal to become more and more like the Carpenter? Sigh.

Okay, so now I know what I must do. But it doesn't make doing it any easier.

The next morning, I look for a chance to speak privately to Karen, but no opportunity arises and it's getting closer to noon, when the conference dismisses. Pity.

As the last presenter begins, I sneak from the meeting hall to check out of my hotel room and take my suitcase to the car to get a jump on the crowd. On my way out of the building, I shoot up a little semi-apologetic, well-I-tried-but-it-didn't-pan-out prayer and add, "Lord, if You want me to say something to Karen, You're going to have to make it happen, because I obviously can't."

Okay. So who do you think is standing just outside on the sidewalk—all alone—checking her phone messages?

I could have gone out any number of doors on three different sides of the hotel, but I exited this one. The one where she happens to be.

Are You kidding me, Lord? Oh man. Now I have to put up or shut up. My compassion has obviously not kicked in yet, but I can't wait on it any longer.

So I take a big bitter bite of humble pie (why does it taste so much like liver?) and, like a puppy with its tail between its legs, I skulk over to Karen. I'm glumly staring at her with my face all blotchy and sweaty when she finally notices me. A very surprised look washes over her. She quickly ends her phone call, and we both just stand there in uncomfortable silence for a long moment.

"Um, Karen, I don't. . ." I begin, then falter. *Okay, Deb, dig deep. Just do it.*

"I want to ask your forgiveness. I call myself a Christian, but I haven't been acting very Christlike toward you. We've been friends far too long to just throw it away over a disagreement. Will you please forgive me for overreacting?"

Frozen, I'd say, is an accurate description of her expression. But, to her credit, Karen defrosts before my eyes and stretches out her arms for a hug. "Oh, Debbie, I'm sorry, too. Of course I'll forgive you. . .if you'll forgive me."

Thankfully, this damaged relationship story has a happy ending. I wish they all did.

Healthy Release

Don't you agree that forgiveness is one of the most difficult things our faith requires of us? Most of us stink at it but, thankfully, it's a skill that improves with practice. Like applying eyeliner. Remember the first few times you tried, you looked like a deranged circus clown?

Well, okay, maybe forgiveness isn't like eyeliner, but it's the same principle: The more we forgive, the more forgiving we become.

When we realize what forgiveness actually does for us, it's a wonder we don't jump to do it more often. Studies have shown that forgiveness decreases stress, depression, and anxiety. But that's really not new news. Back in the sixteenth century, Martin Luther said, "Heavy thoughts bring on physical maladies; when the soul is oppressed, so is the body."

Letting go of our pent-up anger can significantly lower blood pressure, improve cholesterol ratios, and increase cardiovascular efficiency. According to neurosurgeon David Levy, MD, author of *Gray Matter*, "Emotions affect your immune system, for better or worse. Happiness heals like a medicine. Bitterness kills like a disease. Releasing bitterness can dramatically help the underlying causes of many physical ailments."[8]

And besides that, forgiveness is essential to achieve inner peace. Grudges corrode the spirit. But you already know that. The longer we carry around grudges, the more ravenous they become as they devour our passion for life. Resentment is poisonous. The poison gradually spreads throughout every molecule of our being and slowly kills the life spark within us.

Like cancer of the soul.

Robert Muller, former assistant secretary-general of the United Nations, said, "Only the brave know how to forgive. A coward never forgives." I have to agree with that 100 percent. . . . I can't think of anything more courageous than forgiving someone who has caused you harm. Especially on purpose.

Consider the rejected lover who threw acid in the face of a beautiful twenty-six-year-old Iranian woman named Ameneh Bahrami, burning her face so severely that her eyes were destroyed and her skin will forever be brutally scarred. All because she refused to marry him.[9]

Eight years later, this same man was on his knees, sobbing, about to be blinded with acid by a physician, in accordance with Iran's court-ordered "eye-for-an-eye" retribution law. But Ameneh, led into the room by two women, intervened at the last minute, sparing her attacker and forsaking revenge by simply stating, "I forgave him, I forgave him."

Dig Up Those Dead Dogs

But how do we forgive? How do we release our need for revenge and prevent anger, bitterness, and resentment from raking our hearts with their destructive claws?

Well, one thing I've learned: You may not feel forgiving, but if, out of sheer obedience to Christ, you voice your pardon anyway—every day if need be, until it "takes" in your heart—true forgiveness will follow. In other words, feelings often come after the decision to take action. Mark Twain said, "In twenty years, you will be more disappointed by what you didn't do than by what you did."

So why not do it now and save yourself the angst?

My rift with Karen is a good example. Compassion and forgiveness eventually did kick in, but only after I asked her forgiveness in an act of the will. . .not because I felt like it. At the time, I wanted to blowtorch her Wonderbra.

In my book *More Beauty, Less Beast,* I suggest a tool that helps dredge up compassion when the well is bone dry. I call it the Dead Dog Technique. It's simple but incredibly effective. Here's how it works: Imagine that your offender's beloved doggie just died. Even picture the cute little dog. Your offender is so emotionally overwrought that she's lashing out. You've been caught in the backlash. Empathy arises within you (who hasn't experienced the heartache of losing your best furry friend?) and your heart begins to soften toward her. You start seeing her as a vulnerable and feeling person—just like you—who made a forgivable mistake, rather than a cold-blooded, evil person who ruthlessly wounded you.

Honest, it really works. Try it and you'll see.

A friend shared with me another compassion-eliciting technique that works for her: Picture your foe as a sweet little baby. Who can detest an innocent, adorable baby? It truly makes a huge difference when we pray to see our enemy through our Father's eyes. That's how He sees her (just as He sees you and me)—as His beautiful, beloved baby.

If It Was Easy, Everybody Would Do It

*W*hen we're wounded, it's important to take time out to acknowledge our feelings, good, bad, and hideous. Speak the truth, even if your voice cracks. Rather than bust out swinging in a protective knee-jerk reaction, step back to gain a new perspective before responding. Did you catch that? Respond rather than react. There's a big difference. The former is like brewing a cup of tea; the latter is like dropping Mentos in your can of Diet Coke. (Warning: Don't try this at home even if someone double-dog dares you.)

Emotions are wired into us by our passionate Father, who feels things strongly and made us in His image. We were created to feel. The only people who don't feel anger, bitterness, or resentment are dead people. But after we passionately feel, we need to bring those potentially destructive emotions under Christ's submission and not let them run wild.

One way to do this is by writing down your negative feelings. Let them spill out freely—just vomit them all over the page. You might then consider taking it a step further by burning the paper or tying it to a helium balloon and releasing it in a symbolic gesture of letting your anger go. Something about watching that balloon float away on the gentle breeze is incredibly freeing.

Recognize that harboring resentment is like chugging down strychnine and expecting the other person to die. Your anger doesn't hurt your offender. It hurts you. It wounds you and those who care about you, those who feel helpless and hopeless watching bitterness gnaw away like ravenous sewer rats at the you they love. Rats that will never be satiated.

I've heard it said that apologizing doesn't necessarily mean you're wrong and the other person is right. It just means you value relationships more than your ego. And isn't that the way Papa wants us to prioritize?

Forgiveness isn't about changing someone else. You don't have the power to do that. It's about changing something within you. You probably don't have the power to do that either, but you know Someone who does.

Forgiveness is about unlatching the hurt you wear like a heavy, bulletproof lead vest so that you can finally drop it to the floor and feel Papa God's big, loving, beating heart as He embraces you. He forgave you and wants you to do the same for others. "If you forgive others for the wrongs they do to you, your Father in heaven will forgive you. But if you don't forgive others, your Father will not forgive your sins" (Matthew 6:14–15 CEV).

Well, that's pretty plain, isn't it? Forgiveness isn't really optional for believers—in order for us to receive forgiveness, we must give it. Forgiveness is the foundation for an ongoing intimate relationship with our heavenly Father. And He has good reason for issuing this ultimatum.

You can't seethe and love at the same time. You must pick one.

Forgiveness isn't easy. Your offenders may not ever acknowledge—or even know—that they did anything wrong. Or worse, they may know and not care. Those are probably the hardest offenses to let go, but let go we must. Or else our emotional panties will stay perpetually stuck in a wad up yonder where the sun doesn't shine.

Forgetting may not necessarily follow forgiving either, but that's okay. Give it time. Even if you can't forget, you can still forgive anyway. Just don't blame the Big Guy like my girlfriend who says, "Forgiving I can do. . .maybe. . .on a good day. But forgetting? No way! God gave me a great memory. So it's not my fault that I can't forgive and forget—it's His."

Reconciliation with your offender may never happen, but that doesn't mean you can't change your focus from the pain he or she caused you to the healing and wholeness Papa God is performing in you. You can!

I recently read about an eighteen-year-old soldier named Richard Luttrell, who, in a life-or-death combat confrontation with a Vietnamese soldier, squeezed the trigger, taking the life of his enemy. Before he left the scene, Richard removed from the slain soldier a photo of the young Vietnamese man sitting beside a little pigtailed girl, most likely his daughter. Richard carried the photo in his wallet for thirty years, unable to forgive himself for robbing that little girl of her daddy.

Richard returned to North Vietnam years later looking for that little girl, now a young adult. He found her. Returning the picture to her, he begged her forgiveness. She freely gave it to him, releasing his imprisoned heart and returning peace to his tortured soul.[10]

The boots of peace in our armor are far more excellent than any pair of Pradas or Guccis. They never scuff, pinch, or chafe, and they show incredible panache. They're always in style. The comfort they bring isn't just for your arches; it extends to your mind, body, and spirit. And there's only one way to snag these designer boots. Jesus, the Prince of Peace, said, "In Me you may have peace. In the world you have tribulation, but take courage; I have overcome the world" (John 16:33 NASB).

If you want what you do not have,
you must do what you have not done.

UNKNOWN

More Pluck, Less Chicken

1. When growing up, did you have a role model of forgiveness? What did you learn about forgiveness from your family and close friends? Do you have a role model as an adult?

2. Is there someone whose inner peace and capacity for forgiveness you'd like to emulate? (As an example, Google the life story of Corrie ten Boom, one of my personal forgiveness heroes.)

3. What types of offenses are the hardest for you to forgive? To forget? How has Papa God played a part in your successfully resolving any resentment lingering in your heart?

4. What was the most meaningful reconciliation of your life? Who instigated it?

5. Romans 12:14 instructs us, "Ask God to bless everyone who mistreats you. Ask him to bless them and not to curse them" (CEV). Do you tend to hold grudges? Can you think of someone you still haven't forgiven from your childhood? How about from your adult life? What's stopping you from doing that now?

Chapter 14

Fear Not Tomorrow. . .God's Already There
(Shield of Faith: Perseverance)

Do not be afraid or discouraged,
for the Lord will personally go ahead
of you. He will be with you; he will
neither fail you nor abandon you.

DEUTERONOMY 31:8 NLT

I remember well the first time I set eyes on the slim, stylishly dressed young woman with blond-highlighted hair, smiling at me across my hand therapy table. Elizabeth looked more like a hip chick out shopping with girlfriends than a patient who'd come to my occupational therapy clinic for a splint to prevent the fingers of her right hand from balling into a fist.

It was only a few months after a stroke (also called CVA for Cerebral Vascular Accident) had stolen all volitional use of the thirty-four-year-old single mom's right arm and leg, and changed her life forever.

Elizabeth had gone to bed one Friday night with a headache. The next morning, she heard her alarm go off at 8:00 a.m., but she was unable to reach out to turn it off or even call for help. When she didn't show up for breakfast, Elizabeth's eight-year-old son found her unresponsive in bed and called his father (he and Elizabeth had just divorced), who then alerted 911.

The attending police officer erroneously concluded it was a drug overdose, and somehow Elizabeth fell through the cracks. After a stomach contents analysis, which showed no cause for concern, she was left unconscious in the hallway of the busy hospital for twelve hours with only monitoring of her vital signs to make sure she was still alive.

By the time an MRI diagnosed the CVA, it was too late for early-response treatment. Elizabeth was left with short-term memory loss, speaking deficits, and paralysis of her right side. By the time I met her, she had regained much of her speech and was able to hobble along with a leg brace and cane.

During the seven years since the CVA, Elizabeth has learned to walk with a slight limp, dress, bathe, cook, and care for herself and her son, using only her left hand because she still has no use of the right. She depends on compensatory techniques for her quirky short-term memory (which means she might be even more of a sticky-note queen than me) and continues to work as an elementary school media specialist with assistance for lifting and carrying.

She has made the best of a very tough situation. One that makes the rest of us secretly tremble. We'd like to think Elizabeth's is an isolated case. . .that something as horrifyingly life-altering as a stroke doesn't really happen to thirty-four-year-olds. But Elizabeth was one of six individuals enrolled in the Stroke Club I established for under-fifty-five-year-olds. Did you catch that? There were six CVA survivors under the age of fifty-five—three of them under forty—in my small community alone, during one six-month segment of time.

It can happen to anyone. Anytime.

Simmering on the Front Burner

*L*isten, it's not my intention to give you more to fret over, but we all must be aware that debilitating life disruptions—like CVAs—do happen to people of all ages. I recently read that 200,000 people younger than age sixty-five are among the half-million Americans afflicted with Alzheimer's disease.[11] And did you know that each year, three-quarters of a million Americans have their first heart attack?[12] Twenty-nine million polled American women say they've suffered severe physical domestic violence.[13] Hundreds of thousands are treated annually in hospitals for violence-related injuries.

Unforeseen trauma happens to everyone. Faith is not a GET OUT OF JAIL FREE card. (Although it is a GET OUT OF HELL FREE card!) "Your Father in heaven. . .gives his sunlight to both the evil and the good, and he sends rain on the just and the unjust alike" (Matthew 5:45 NLT).

According to my fear survey, debilitating injury or disability is a front-burner worry many of us have (it was number 2, falling only behind losing a loved one). Old age/senility was pretty high, too, at number 4; and dependency on others, a common by-product of debilitating illness, ranked seventh. It appears that fears related to losing our health and abilities weigh heavily on the minds of a lot of us.

It's a simmering fear we know could happen. In fact, we dread that it might. We can't imagine how we could possibly endure if catastrophic illness or injury should permanently alter our bodies or our lifestyles. We find comfort in the familiar. Change often seems terrifying.

It does the heart good to know that some people can rise above fear and intentionally risk loss of their health (or even their lives) for the good of others. Like Mother Teresa and her work with the lepers in India. Or Grandma Jesse, my friend Sandi's grandmother, who voluntarily took care of dozens of neighbors quarantined with smallpox in the 1930s while raising her own sixteen children plus five adopted orphans.

Both were women who trusted that their shields of faith would protect them as they ministered to others as Christ's hands and feet on earth. But sometimes, as hard as it is for us to understand, Papa God allows our health and lifestyles to change. When that happens, it takes perseverance to continue moving forward in the wake of that change.

I Will Survive!

I asked Elizabeth and my friend Kathleen, who lost the use of half her body ten years ago due to a stroke at age fifty-seven, their secrets of successfully persevering—of embracing a new normal—while continuing to grow spiritually. Both are ordinary people who have become extraordinary women of beauty, faith, and joy and who, with their positive attitudes, uplift and inspire those around them. I believe the wisdom in their answers applies not just to stroke survivors, but to survivors of other life-altering circumstances as well. And, you know, that would be all of us sooner or later, wouldn't it?

- Develop a support system. Seek the company of those dealing with similar challenges. Online and live support groups help you problem-solve (someone has probably already figured out a way to do that thing you can't) and offer understanding in a way no one else can. Elizabeth says, "At first, I didn't know anybody like me. . .but there are lots of us and when we get together, we're just normal people." Families are a natural support system if they're available, but if not blood family, establish a spirit-family that will faithfully hold up your needs in prayer. Special-interest groups add zest and a new dimension to your world as well. After her stroke, Kathleen joined the Joy Group at her church for ages fifty-five-plus and became very active in her local DAR chapter (Daughters of the American Revolution). Whatever you do, don't isolate yourself.

- Pay attention to what God is doing. Elizabeth confides, "I truly, truly believe that God got my attention by the stroke. I was a stagnant baby Christian for four years before the CVA, and then one day several months afterward, I was reading the gospel of John and suddenly I woke up spiritually. My relationship with God has grown deeper ever since. I now feel that the Lord is calling me to minister to disabled kids and adults who are alone, detached, and need support from someone who's been there. In a way, the stroke is the best thing that ever happened to me. I'm no longer afraid of dying. I know where I'm going—to heaven—and I know He's going to take me when the time is right and not a minute before."

- Personal restoration. Reenergize when you're depleted. Watch a funny movie, laugh, sing, sit in a garden, pump it up with great music, do something you love. It may take a little more time and energy to do things than it used to, so it's very important to refill your tank on a daily basis.

- Discover your new self. Elizabeth was a self-described overachiever before the CVA. "I've discovered my different self; not a worse self, just a different self. Sure, there are some things I can't do. . .run with my son, dance, thread a needle. But I try to focus on the things I can do and enjoy those. God gives me each day, and it's up to me to make them happy."

- Give yourself time. Elizabeth admits that motivation can be slow in coming. "At first I was living only for my son, but after renewing my relationship with Christ, I began to live for me." Kathleen learned that acceptance of your new lifestyle doesn't happen overnight. "If I had known ten years ago that I'd be in a wheelchair the rest of my life, I would have crumbled. But God, in His wisdom, said, 'I'll introduce you gradually to this process,' and now the chair doesn't stop me—it gets me where I want to go."

- Explore new ways of doing things. After trying to make spaghetti for the first time, Elizabeth was petrified of cooking. Imagine yourself going through the entire spaghetti-making process with your right hand tied behind your back and you can empathize. But takeout every night was too expensive. So she sought help from an occupational therapist who came to her house, assessed her needs, and recommended great new adaptive ways of doing things. Now she cooks for herself and her son all the time. Fear diminishes as understanding increases.

- Adjust your expectations of yourself and your world. Downsize your sphere of influence, let go of your old performance pressure, and set new personal goals. What is one thing you want to accomplish today? This week? This year? According to Kathleen, you must become a good "waiter" as you patiently wait on the Lord to show you what kind of miracle He will work in and for you.

- Impact another life. "Encourage one another and build each other up" (1 Thessalonians 5:11 NIV). Intentionally encourage the people you come in contact with—the mailman, the cleaning lady, the exterminator. Kathleen advises taking an active interest in the people who serve you in any capacity and letting them know they're important to you. Pray for them and let them know you're lifting them up in prayer. "Take your eyes off yourself and focus on them. Make them feel that someone really cares about them. I thank them constantly and try to remember to ask about their families and what's important to them." Elizabeth agrees: "There are so many people who don't feel good about themselves—take it upon yourself to help them feel better."

- Savor the little things. Kathleen is one of the most humbly thankful people I know. "Since my CVA, I wake up in the morning just glad to be alive. I'm very thankful for the little things. . . I dressed myself today! Another thing you can do is to learn to appreciate good food—it really can be comfort food. Just eating out at good restaurants once a month keeps me going and gives me something to look forward to. That's something people can do for their disabled friends—take them out to eat once a month. You can't imagine how much it will mean to them." Kathleen also suggests, "Live one day at a time and savor the things—especially the little things—that bring you pleasure. Like a sparrow singing at your window, a scampering kitten, a refreshing bite of watermelon, a new picture of your grandbaby, or having lunch with a friend."

- Cultivate hope. Kathleen advises communicating daily with cheerful people; project a positive attitude to others and yourself by wearing bright colors and immersing yourself in spiritually uplifting books, music, or movies. Break out wonderful family memories with old photo albums, CDs, or videos; reliving them will open the door to hope for the future. Exercise your brain (playing bridge, working puzzles, doing Sudoku). "Depend on God's grace to calm your fears. Keep your mind active and your spirit growing—that's the key to hope and a positive outlook."

It is possible to not just survive, but thrive after debilitating illness turns your world upside down. Kathleen and Elizabeth are just two of many terrific examples of people whose perseverance through their weakest moments points to Papa God's strength.

People who pray not that the Lord would lessen their loads, but that He would give them stronger backs.

People who wear their shields of faith as protection against the onslaught of fear, defeat, and depression.

People who are true heroes because they live out loud every minute of every day and have actually become the ideal to which we all aspire: victorious. "We often suffer, but we are never crushed. Even when we don't know what to do, we never give up" (2 Corinthians 4:8 CEV).

To fear is one thing. To let fear grab you by the tail and swing you around is another.

KATHERINE PATERSON

More Pluck, Less Chicken

1. Is debilitating injury or illness on the front burner of your fear list?

2. Name three people you know who have risen above debilitation to accomplish great things. Some high-profile examples are Joni Eareckson Tada, a multitalented artist who has been a quadriplegic for four decades since breaking her neck as a teen (www.joniandfriends.org), and Nick Jujicic, an amazing Australian preacher whose motto is "No limbs. No limits" (www.lifewithoutlimbs.org). Hey, if you need a shot of raw inspiration, check out these incredible examples of perseverance!

3. You may not be dealing with life-altering debilitation, but no doubt there are traumas that you must persevere through. Which of the ten suggestions by Elizabeth and Kathleen can you adapt to your own situation to help you become a victor?

4. How does this assurance from James 1:12 infuse hope into the trials you are now facing? "Blessed is the one who perseveres under trial because, having stood the test, that person will receive the crown of life that the Lord has promised to those who love him" (NIV).

5. Stop for a moment and pray for someone you know who is struggling to persevere through a difficult time. Why not share this chapter with them? Perhaps they, too, will be inspired by humble conquerors like Elizabeth, Kathleen, Joni, and Nick.

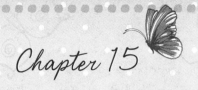

Chapter 15

This Helmet Is Worth Hat Hair
(Helmet of Salvation: Grace)

God's grace has set us free.

ROMANS 6:15 NLT

$\mathcal{I}$t was just after midnight when my friend Michael parked his patrol car six yards behind another sheriff's deputy who had pulled over someone for a traffic violation. The red and blue lights on both cruisers were whirling when Michael arrived as backup for his fellow officer, who was standing at the driver's window of the violator's vehicle parked in front of the two patrol cars on the side of the highway.

Michael opened his car door, climbed out, and was just taking his second step away from the vehicle when suddenly his world exploded.

Without warning, a drunk driver going fifty miles per hour slammed into the back of Michael's patrol car without once touching her brakes. The thirty-something woman, who had just left a bar, later said she never saw the flashing lights. The impact sent Michael's car smashing into the patrol car in front of his, which then plowed into the car in front of it. Both patrol cars were totaled and the civilian vehicles were heavily damaged. Thanks to the good Lord and air bags, no one was seriously injured.

As Michael, stunned and white-faced, surveyed the heap of smoldering, twisted metal that only moments before had cradled his past, present, and future, the what-ifs began bombarding his mind.

What if his patrol car hadn't been there to absorb the initial impact? No doubt the other officer and driver in the pulled-over car would have perished.

What if the drunk driver had hit Michael's cruiser five seconds earlier? Michael would have been either inside this now-crumpled mass of destruction or, worse, halfway out. The truth sank in. He had been moments away from dying on his son's first birthday.

What if the drunk driver had seen Michael's patrol car at the last second and swerved to miss it? She would have nailed Michael head-on as he stood beside his door.

The what-ifs made Michael's blood run cold. (More about the what-ifs in chapter 18.) The possibilities were terrifying. It was at that moment he came face-to-face with the true, ineffable meaning of grace.

By definition, grace is unmerited divine assistance. Undeserved favor. An act of kindness originating from God.

Michael had been saved by grace. There were many reasons why he should have died in that wreck, but only one reason that he lived. Unmerited divine assistance. . .an act of kindness from the hand of the Almighty. Although Michael had done nothing to deserve it, he would once again witness a beautiful sunrise, kiss his wife good morning, and hold his precious baby in his arms.

Grace Tattoo

In the same way Michael was physically saved by grace, we can be spiritually saved by grace: "Those who receive the abundance of grace and of the gift of righteousness will reign in life through the One, Jesus Christ" (Romans 5:17 NASB).

We've done nothing to deserve it. There are many reasons why we should die in our sin-wrecked lives, but only one reason we're offered life after life. And that reason is grace. Jesus Christ loves us so much that He died in our place so that we, too, could triumph with Him as champions over death, sin, and ultimate destruction.

Okay, girlfriend, clear your head (helps me to shake mine like a wet dog, but watch out for flying saliva). Read this next paragraph slowly, considering every word.

Sin didn't, and doesn't, have a chance in competition with the aggressive forgiveness we call grace. *When it's sin versus grace, grace wins hands down. All sin can do is threaten us with death, and that's the end of it. Grace, because God is putting everything together again through the Messiah, invites us into life.*

ROMANS 5:20–21 MSG (EMPHASIS MINE)

Don't you just want to tattoo that incredible scripture right across your chest? (If yours is the size of mine, the words would wrap all the way around your back and down to your derriere dimples.)

Even after we make bad choices, grace invites us back into life. It won't leave us dead and rotting. It gives us the re-opportunity to live life to the fullest. Because grace, that "aggressive forgiveness" (I just love that phrase!), trumps sin. Any sin. And Papa God is already gluing the shattered pieces of the mess we've made of ourselves back together through the love of Jesus.

Are you feeling the bigness of this, sister?

There's that ding-dang tear trickling down my cheek again. Seriously. Aggressive forgiveness does it to me every time. Sniff.

In writing this book, I interviewed dozens and dozens of people about their fears and how faith provides courage. Grace plays a large part in that. I've continually run across accounts like Michael's, demonstrating how grace is instrumental in salvaging potential disaster. The stories are downright mind-blowing.

Take, for instance, Nancy, a poet, whose all-consuming fears culminated in a catatonic state. She couldn't talk. She couldn't move. It was like living death. Nancy graciously shared with me an intensely moving poem that contains these illuminating passages about this dark chapter of her life:

> *I climbed into myself one day for*
> > *safety and protection.*
> *Soon I found that I was trapped. . .*
> > *a script that had no plot.*

Oh man. I can identify with Nancy's lostness, can't you? I hope the final verse of Nancy's poem speaks grace to your heart like it did mine:

> *The maze was complicated,*
> > *and fear was always there;*
> *I wasn't even able to turn to God in prayer.*
> *But though I couldn't form the words,*
> > *my spirit called in pain,*
> *And slowly I returned to life out from*
> > *that dark domain.*
> *Although the memory of this will always be in me,*

*My Lord has given peace and strength,
and now I'm living. . .free!*

Grace Really Is Amazing

And then there's Amanda, a young escapee from an abusive marriage, whose heart's desire was to have a baby with her second husband, a Christ-follower. When cancerous cells were detected on her cervix, her options were cryosurgery (freezing and cutting off the cancer) or a hysterectomy, which of course would close the door to pregnancy. There was no guarantee that the first option wouldn't lock the maternity door either, but after much prayer, Amanda chose cryosurgery.

Sadly, it wasn't successful. The cancer persisted. Her physician recommended a hysterectomy. Amanda's family and friends urged her toward that procedure. Her own fears clamored for it. But Amanda prayed and prayed. What did the Lord want?

Against all logic and medical advice, she felt led to try cryosurgery again. In Amanda's own words, "I was lying on the table, praying with my husband. The doctor came in and started to prepare me for the very uncomfortable procedure. Suddenly he stopped, removed his scope, and said, 'There are no cancer cells. They're completely gone.' The malignancy was there one minute and gone the next with no medical explanation. It was purely the power of God."

Several years later Amanda gave birth to a healthy, nine-pound, five-ounce baby boy, thanking Papa God for His grace with every inch of her heart.

My friend Marianna is another example of someone saved by grace. One evening when she was four years old, Marianna returned home from buying takeout dinner with her father. While her dad began setting the table, Marianna ran upstairs to get her mom and found her mother's lifeless body hanging from the rafters.

In those days, the late fifties, suicide was not something you talked about. Ever. The acceptable societal strategy was for Marianna's father, church friends, neighbors, and extended family to grieve privately and then move on with their lives. No one considered the consequences of painful silence to a confused, heartbroken little girl who thought she was the cause of her mother's death; that her mother must have been extremely disappointed in her only child to feel driven to kill herself.

Marianna could have folded in upon herself and shriveled away from grief, self-loathing, and blame. But she gave her heart to Jesus at age eleven and from that day on, by Papa God's grace, she grew up comforted by the knowledge that although things don't always make sense, the Lord is in control, and we are safe in His hands.

That's not to say that Marianna didn't sometimes rail in anger at what might have been. She did. But grace carried her through those hard times. "I think it all boils down to: Who are we going to trust?" Marianna shared with me in her soft voice. "God knows exactly what we think and feel. Peace comes in accepting the path He's set out for us and realizing that none of it was done to hurt us or make us miserable. We have to trust that He'll fill in the holes."

You know, it's no coincidence that the piece of spiritual armor representing salvation through grace is a helmet. We need sturdy, impenetrable headgear to protect our thoughts, reasoning, and motives from the destructive fear of potential disaster. That thick brain padding in our helmet is the assurance that through life, death, or near misses, we're safe in Papa God's hands.

And that's worth helmet hair any day.

*The wise man in the storm prays
to God, not for safety from danger,
but for deliverance from fear.*

RALPH WALDO EMERSON

More Pluck, Less Chicken

1. Can you recall a time when you were physically saved by the grace of Papa God?

2. Have you been spiritually saved by grace? When?

3. Flip back a few pages and read Romans 5:20–21 aloud. What part of that passage resonates most with you?

4. Do you have any tattoos? (Just kidding! You don't have to answer that one.) But, hey, what scripture tat would you choose if you had one—the one verse you'd like to keep close to your heart always?

5. Which holes has Papa God filled in your life through His grace?

Chapter 16

Stained-Glass Warrior
(The Sword of the Spirit: God's Word)

*You don't need to be afraid of the dark
any more, nor fear the dangers of the day.*

PSALM 91:5 TLB

~

Oh no! They're leaving me—I'll be all alone up here! As I lay
sprawled like a rag doll on the Rocky Mountain slope, my heart
sank while I watched the tiny, gliding figures of my teenage son
and daughter disappear around the bend of the ski run. They had
no way of knowing that the tumble I had just taken down the
frozen slope had wrecked my knee. They thought Mom would
just bounce back up and keep going. . .as always.

Not this time.

The pop-pop I felt when my ski skidded on a patch of ice
was accompanied by a stab of pain. After I'd rolled head over
heels to a discombobulated stop, I gathered my wits (which
were strewn all over the hard-packed slope) and tried to stand.
Ye-ouch! I felt the bones in my knee separate and had to use
my hands to push my upper and lower leg back into vertical
alignment.

Dr. Deb's astute diagnosis: ruptured knee ligaments. Serious
trouble.

I flopped back down, sitting in the thick snow, a cold hard knot of fear forming in the pit of my stomach. It was roughly an hour before sundown, the slopes were deserted, and no one was even aware that I was hurt. What was I supposed to do now?

A sharp wind began to blow as deep shadows slanted across the face of the mountain. As the minutes crept by, my behind started to feel like a frozen rump roast, and I became acutely aware of my proximity to the edge of the darkening forest. Why did it make me so nervous? I couldn't tear my eyes away from the dense brush and trees ten yards away.

Then the memory of a sign posted above our table at lunch in the ski lodge hit me like a jolt of electricity: COUGAR ALERT! Our server explained that during the winter months, hungry cougars sometimes wander into populated areas, searching for food, and there had been several recent attacks. Just last week, a woman had been killed while cross-country skiing.

Gulp. And here I was—a wounded sitting duck. I pictured my rescuers finding only the shredded remains of my parka scattered across the ski slope. An uncontrollable shivering began deep in my gut and gradually spread over my entire body. I seized my ski pole and pointed it shakily toward the woods.

As if that would do any good if a cougar came shopping for dinner.

What I needed was a sword. A weapon. Something powerful that would keep my mortal enemy from ripping helpless, defenseless me into itsy-bitsy pieces.

My knee began to throb, so I packed snow around it and realized I could no longer feel my fingers or toes. My face felt like an ice mask. I sat there in the frozen stillness, feeling completely and utterly alone.

My eyes drifted toward the mountaintops across the deep valley in front of me and beheld an incredible sight. The sun was setting behind the highest peaks, casting vibrant crimson streaks across the sky like the fingers of a vast hand reaching out.... Why, those fingers were reaching right out to me!

A Bible verse I'd learned long ago sprang to mind: "I lift up my eyes to the mountains—where does my help come from? My help comes from the LORD, the Maker of heaven and earth" (Psalm 121:1–2 NIV). I said the verse aloud again and again. The words seemed to take on a life of their own, growing richer and mightier and more vibrant each time.

Then a strange and marvelous thing happened. The majesty of the mountaintop scene consumed me, and a warm, quiet peace filled my heart. I realized that I had indeed been given a sword—a powerful weapon that would keep fear, my immortal enemy, from ripping my helpless, defenseless heart into itsy-bitsy pieces.

Verse after verse started popping into my head, some from my childhood, some more recently memorized, some I thought were long forgotten. Like old friends, they surrounded and comforted me.

- When I am afraid, I put my trust in you. (Psalm 56:3 NIV)

- "Be strong and courageous! Do not tremble or be dismayed, for the LORD your God is with you wherever you go." (Joshua 1:9 NASB)

- "Don't be afraid.... Take courage! I am here!" (Mark 6:50 NLT)

- God is our refuge and strength, an ever-present help in trouble. (Psalm 46:1 NIV)

- Don't be afraid. I am with you. Don't tremble with fear. I am your God. I will make you strong, as I protect you with my arm and give you victories. (Isaiah 41:10 CEV)

The ski-patrol guys who eventually found me wondered why

I asked them to snap a photo of me before bundling me onto the rescue sled. "Are you sure this is a memory you want to keep?" one asked as he eyed my blue lips and swollen knee.

"Absolutely," I replied with assurance. "I want to always remember the day I learned to swordfight."

To this day I smile every time I see that picture. Certainly not because of the three surgeries necessary to put my knee back together, but because of the faith-bolstering lesson my Father taught me when He had my full attention up on that frigid mountain. (If you'd like to see the photo, hop over to my website www.DeboraCoty.com and click on "About Me" and then "Last Ski Run.")

I'm a firm believer in the mega-importance of keeping a full arsenal of scripture loaded and ready for battle. God's Word is our sword—our biggest and best weapon. We never know when or where the enemy will ambush us, and we won't always have a Bible, our pastor, or our trusty notes handy. We might have only a frozen rump. Our sword must be mobile, sharp, and handy at all times. Even on a lonely mountaintop.

Build Your Arsenal

Okay, don't panic if your ammo is a little anemic in the scripture memory department—stocking up is not as hard as you might think. Invest an hour in ferreting out a dozen pithy verses you want to memorize (you can find a bunch right here in this book!). Then jot them on index cards or put them on your smartphone or tablet. Keep them in your purse to review in those stare-at-the-ceiling moments when you're killing time waiting for someone or something.

Make your goal one new verse per week, but if it takes two weeks to memorize one, don't sweat it. Repeat the verse aloud every time you climb in your car or stop at a red light. Pull it out during downtimes throughout the day and let it be the last thing you see before going to bed. You'll be surprised how quickly it starts to take root in your brain.

Many verses have been put to music by various artists over the years. Do an online search and download praise songs containing your targeted verses. Or create your own melody! Singing words makes them stick better.

By the end of six months, you'll have all twelve verses nailed. You'll be proud of you, Papa God will be proud of you, and I'll be proud of you, too!

Two years ago, I became convicted that I needed to spend more daily time in the Word. Oh, it wasn't that I hadn't been reading scripture; I was actually pretty good about studying books of the Bible, a few verses here, a chapter there. . .when I had time. But I wanted more. I wanted Papa God to be able to depend on me as faithfully as I depend on Him.

So I resolved to read, study, and meditate on scripture every single day, seven days a week. Not because I had to. Not so I could check my accomplishment off on some righteous to-do list. But because I wanted to. My reason was simple: I knew the Word is one of the primary ways Papa God speaks to us, and I didn't want to miss anything!

You know what? That decision has been the most edifying, beautifying, fulfilling decision of my life. I've heard something new and fresh and totally applicable from my Savior's still, small voice every day for the past two years. Scripture has become my life-map, my guide, like a personal GPS (God-Powered Satellite). I use a variety of translations (my favorite is a side-by-side version of the New International Version translation and *The Message*) and keep a Bible dictionary and several commentaries handy for clarification when questions arise.

Prepare to Attack

*H*ey, did you realize that the sword is the only piece of the armor of God that is an overtly offensive weapon? All the other armor components (shield, helmet, breastplate, chain mail, and boots) are primarily for defense and protection against assaults on us. The sword (scripture) is our designated weapon to aggressively attack and disarm our opponent. What kind of wimpy warriors would we be if all we could do is defend ourselves? We need to be willing and able to turn the tables and attack. I mean, really, who wants to be whiney Olive Oyl when you can be big, bad, bold Xena, the Warrior Princess?

But you can't use a sword properly until you can get a good grip on it. In the fray of battle, a flimsy, fumbling grip will only get you killed.

I loved the illustration about this very point that I heard from Pastor Blake Albritton at my parents' church, First Baptist Church of Starke, Florida. Pastor Blake flashed the outline of a hand overhead as he recited the following statistics and pointed to each finger, beginning with the smallest:

We retain only 15 percent of scripture we hear in church (or through media) once a week. That's equivalent to trying to grip our sword with only the pinkie. It would be pretty much impossible. . .way too easy to drop that heavy steel, or for the enemy to knock it away with a well-placed blow. Using only one finger, we lack strength, control, and steadiness to use the sword in the way it was intended.

We have 30 percent retention of what we hear and read. That would be like grasping the sword with our ring finger and pinkie—better but still pretty weak. Not at all dependable in one-on-one combat.

If we include studying with reading and hearing the Word,

we retain roughly 60 percent, which adds the long finger to the ring and pinkie in wielding that sword. Using three fingers, our grip is definitely stronger but we still lack maneuverability and we're bound to fatigue quickly.

When we add memorizing scripture to the other three, the strong index finger (Mr. Pointer to us moms) joins in to create a much sturdier grasp. We now have roughly 90 percent retention. However, we still can't manipulate our sword optimally without a thumb on the handle to counterbalance and stabilize.

Meditating is the thumb. Meditating means marinating in, chewing on, soaking up the meaning of scripture. Once we add that final 10 percent, we're fully equipped to pierce the heart of the enemy with the most effective offensive weapon there is. "For the word of God is living and active and sharper than any two-edged sword" (Hebrews 4:12 NASB).

Our grasp will be unwavering despite blows we may have to ward off because our grip on the Word is sound, well balanced, and firm.

My friend Lynn discovered this when she endured eighteen surgeries, developed over twenty horribly painful kidney stones, was diagnosed with ulcerative colitis and multiple sclerosis, and nearly died from pulmonary emboli when she was six months' pregnant.

Okay, wait—overload. Let me start from the beginning.

Poor health was an alien concept to Lynn, who until age twenty-eight was an extremely fit troupe belly dancer, full-time occupational therapist, and instructor of yoga and Pilates. During those young adult years, Lynn went through the motions of attending church with what she calls an "I-am-in-control-here-but-does-God-need-a-secretary?" attitude. While she was, in her words, "practicing for real faith," Lynn was there in body but not in spirit, never once hearing Papa God speak to her or considering the pursuit of a relationship with Jesus Christ.

But Lynn suddenly found her spiritual eyes opened shortly after her marriage. She got involved in a Spirit-filled church and began feverishly taking notes and identifying with the Bible in ways she never had before. She accepted Christ as her Savior and started walking closely with Him by praying and reading scripture.

About that time, she began experiencing searing abdominal pain and was diagnosed with ulcerative colitis. Along came the first seven surgeries. Then the MS was discovered. Soon afterward, she became pregnant and despite the agonizing passing of dozens of kidney stones and barely surviving bilateral pulmonary emboli, Lynn felt the Lord's grace and peace sustain both her and her unborn baby.

As Lynn studied her Bible and her soul filled with the Word of God, instead of starting the day with pain and worry, she started it with "I can do all things through Him who strengthens me" (Philippians 4:13 NASB). This verse became her mantra.

Although she literally stared down death when, after an emergency C-section to deliver her son, pelvic hematomas required multiple blood transfusions, more surgery, and separation from her newborn for weeks on end, Lynn gripped her sword with all her might. Second Corinthians 4:16, 18 became her lifeline: "We do not lose heart. Though outwardly we are wasting away, yet inwardly we are being renewed day by day. . . . So we fix our eyes not on what is seen, but on what is unseen, since what is seen is temporary, but what is unseen is eternal" (NIV).

Lynn leaves a Bible opened to this special passage at all times and leans heavily on it to get her through days when the simplest things are a battle. By doing so, Lynn intentionally releases her grip on her own control and instead wraps her fingers tightly around her sword.

Fencing Is Not Just for Cow Pastures

$\mathcal{D}$id I mention that Lynn is my supervisor at the rehab company where I work as a therapist? Most people have no idea of Lynn's fragile health because she never complains. Honest. I worked with her for over a year before I caught on.

Far from whining, Lynn shares her effervescent joy with her patients, those of us blessed to be coworkers, and her family. When I asked about her incredible attitude despite severe hip and back pain, covert runs to the bathroom with colitis issues, and chronic fatigue, this was her answer: "Do you remember that excitement you felt as a child when you were going to Disney World, or when you woke up on Christmas morning? Every morning since I left the hospital after my son, Logan, was born, I have woken with that kind of joy. The Lord gives His joy to me, new every morning. It's a blessing and a gift."

And so is Lynn. How blessed am I to be gifted with a swordfighter as a boss?

I hope you have a Lynn in your life. She reminds me of Westley's memorable line in *The Princess Bride* when he likens fencing master Inigo Montoya to a stained-glass window. Inigo displays such magnificent mastery of his sword, it's like viewing a priceless masterpiece. Inigo's grip is solid, his skill level is high, and his confidence is sure.

Because he's had lots of practice.

Does that describe you as you wield your sword?

That's what we should all aspire to be: stained-glass warriors. Unique and unforgettable master swordfighters who constantly practice to ensure that our grip on the Word is solid, our skill level high, and our confidence sure. Whether our enemy lashes out at us as a mortal cougar or immortal fear.

*A champion is someone who
gets up when he can't.*

JACK DEMPSEY, BOXING HEAVYWEIGHT CHAMPION
OF THE WORLD, 1919–1926

More Pluck, Less Chicken

1. Can you recall a time in your life when scripture became your lifeline?

2. Consider the five fingers that grasp the sword of God's Word: hearing, reading, studying, memorizing, and meditating on scripture. Do you need to strengthen your grip in any of these areas?

3. Go back to the beginning of this chapter and read aloud Psalm 91:5. What are your fears of the night and dangers of the day? In what ways can Papa God's living and active Word, sharper than a two-edged sword (see Hebrews 4:12), help you triumph over them?

4. Do you ever feel that like Lynn, you're "practicing for real faith" instead of practicing real faith? What do you think is the difference?

5. Who is the stained-glass warrior in your life? In whose life are you a stained-glass warrior?

Section 4:

Faceless Fears

Bogeymen Love the Dark

Don't be afraid of those who threaten you.
For the time is coming when everything
that is covered will be revealed, and all
that is secret will be made known to all.

MATTHEW 10:26 NLT

Chapter 17

Life after Financial Death
(Money)

Don't fall in love with money.

HEBREWS 13:5 CEV

❧

*M*y friend Georgia understands some of what Lazarus must have gone through in the dark days before Jesus stood in front of Lazarus's tomb, overthrew the forces of death and destruction, and commanded, "Come forth" (John 11:43 KJV).

You see, Georgia also experienced death and lived to tell about it. Not physical death, no. . .financial death. But in a lot of ways, to Georgia it felt very much the same.

Georgia had been a stay-at-home mother of two boys for a decade when her husband, Ron, lost the position in which he'd faithfully labored for nearly twenty years. There was no warning—in fact, Georgia and Ron thought Ron's new boss had requested a meeting to give him a promotion. Instead, Ron was dismissed.

Night after sleepless night, Georgia earnestly prayed that one of Ron's résumés would produce a job offer, but it didn't happen. Georgia was able to land a position selling promotional products, but her income wasn't nearly enough to keep the family afloat. Months passed as she helplessly watched their bank account dry up. By the end of the second year, all their savings, 401k, college funds, stocks, and credit cards had disappeared. In Georgia's words, "It felt like we were in the deepest part of the ocean where the creatures are beyond scary."

Despite Georgia's constant prayers, petitions, and fasting, five long years passed as they struggled through Ron's unemployment and continued to faithfully serve the Lord with the meager resources they had. All she could hear in answer to her pleas for help was Papa God's still, small voice reply, "I'm working."

And He was. Although it didn't appear that way to perplexed neighbors and friends who would ask, "How in the world are you guys making it?" Even during the driest of months, God's grace was evident. Georgia admits, "The miracles were nothing short of amazing."

Like the time Ron's old company called and said they'd found that they still owed him four thousand dollars and would drop a check in the mail that day. And the fact that during the entire five years, their lively, growing boys were never sick or had any accidents that needed medical attention. Or the unexpected large tax return that just had to be a mistake. . .but wasn't. Then there was the donated car. And the time the neighbor boy appeared with perfectly sized, barely worn sneakers for eight-year-old Mark, two days after he wore a hole in his only pair. And the acquaintance (not even a close friend) who stopped by with loaded bags from the Honey Baked Ham shop where she worked.

Still, it wasn't enough. Georgia and Ron could no longer afford the mortgage on their home, so it was sold in a short sale. Ron struggled off and on with depression, hopelessness, and anger toward God. Their marriage was severely strained and at times they both felt desperate—questioning their faith, wondering if God even cared.

There seemed to be no end in sight.

Then, at the five-year-and-nine-month mark of their unemployment faith journey, Ron was offered a job. It was a relatively low-paying, entry-level position but, praise the Lord, it was a job! They were finally able to live within their means and pay their bills on time.

Georgia's story is a reminder of the volatile economic times in which we live. Many people have lost their jobs, their livelihoods, and their financial security.

The roller-coaster stock market feeds fear, leaving many people teetering on the brink of financial disaster. Old and young, men and women, home owners and homeless of every race stand together in food stamp lines. Plunging stocks and dismal 401k statements increase personal debt and cast a dark purple haze over the future. Deep financial scars create deep fears. Retirement, which once promised peace, now threatens distress.

Our prospects look grim. Where can we find hope?

Management versus Ownership

*Y*ou may not realize it, but finances are important to Papa God, too. There are more than two thousand Bible verses about money and possessions. So we can be assured that He cares about the ins and outs of our economic situations (especially when there are more outs than ins).

When talking about money and what it buys, I think the first premise we must establish is that what little—or much—we own isn't really ours in the first place. We're just caretakers. "The earth and everything on it belong to the Lord" (Psalm 24:1 cev). So although the bank account, trust fund, or mortgage might display our name, we're not the real owner. Papa God is.

This is important to grasp from the beginning, so that our perspective stays focused on honoring the Lord with His possessions, the resources that He gives us the responsibility— and privilege—to manage. That means not looking at our belongings as mine, mine, mine. We don't even realize we're doing it, but sometimes, especially when we're threatened with losing them, we do tend to hoard our things and clutch them to our chests, afraid to part with one single molecule.

Did a scripture passage just jump into your head as you read that last paragraph? Read it again and see what memory is tugged. Yes, it's the parable of the talents in Matthew 25.

> *A man went away and put his three servants in charge of all he owned. The man knew what each servant could do. So he handed five thousand coins to the first servant, two thousand to the second, and one thousand to the third. Then he left the country.*
>
> *As soon as the man had gone, the servant with the five thousand coins used them to earn five thousand more. The servant who had two thousand coins did the same with his money and earned two thousand more. But the servant with one thousand coins dug a hole and hid his master's money in the ground.*
>
> VERSES 14–18 (CEV)

So far in the parable, the master (God) has delegated his own money to three caretakers, divided into quantities that he knows they can handle based on his intimate knowledge of each individual. Two of them fulfilled their master's expectations and made him very proud. "I left you in charge of only a little, but now I will put you in charge of much more" (verses 21, 23 CEV).

But one doesn't. He buries his pile like a dead skunk.

Now why would he do that? we wonder.

But maybe we do the same thing. It's called fear. We're afraid to lose what we have, so we hoard and hide, stockpile and stash, and in the process become miserable misers. Like wild lionesses guarding the last shred of zebra carcass, we snarl and fight and claw to hold on to our possessions. Whose possessions? Our possessions.

Why? Because deep down inside, we don't believe the Lord is actually in control, and if we don't defend what's ours, no one will.

You know, Papa isn't taken by surprise when adversity comes our way. Nor should we be. Take a look at James 1:2–3: "Consider it a sheer gift, friends, when tests and challenges come at you from all sides. You know that under pressure, your faith-life is forced into the open and shows its true colors" (MSG).

Notice that passage doesn't say *if* trials come your way, it says *when*. It's a given, girlfriend. It doesn't mean you've done something wrong. It doesn't mean you're being punished. Verse 4 goes on to say that we must endure these rough patches in order to become spiritually mature. Adversity is a necessary part of the growing process.

It's kind of like having to endure labor and delivery to achieve motherhood. At the time it seems like the worst thing in the world, and you're positive you won't live through the ordeal. But in the end, you realize that going through the worst produced the best thing in the world: new life.

Feeding Faith Starves Fear

The old adage is true: That which doesn't kill us makes us stronger. Here's some make-us-stronger advice from Georgia and others who've passed through the valley of the shadow of financial death.

- Don't give up hope. Remember that even when your faith tank (like your gas tank) is empty, your God will remain faithful to you (see 2 Timothy 2:13).

- Separate your needs from your wants. Sometimes we get confused and pray for a Mercedes when what we really need is a bicycle. But Yahweh, Master of all things great and small, knows the difference. "You can be sure that God will take care of everything you *need*" (Philippians 4:19 MSG, emphasis mine).

- Sweeten your bitter words. You might have to eat them one day. Despite the temptation to bad-mouth your circumstances, choose to take the high road. Don't dwell on the unfairness of your poverty or trash that lousy, rotten ex-boss who laid you off. Be careful what you say. Be careful what you think.

- There's good reason why Philippians 4:8 instructs us to "fix your thoughts on what is true, and honorable, and right" (NLT). Not only is negativity directly correlated to heart disease, immune system deficits, and our ability to cope with pain (and heaven knows we need more of that), but negative words from our mouths internalize into negative attitudes, which paint our vision black. We need to step out of the darkroom of fear into the light. That's how we destroy all our negatives. "Words kill, words give life; they're either poison or fruit—you choose" (Proverbs 18:21 MSG).

- Keep communication lines open. "Pray without ceasing" (1 Thessalonians 5:17 NASB). Talk to your heavenly Father—

tell Him your frustrations, fears, and failures. Go ahead—pound on His chest and sob. He can take it. He's a very big God. Then dry your tears and thank Him for the blessings that you do have, and that things are not worse. If you don't believe they could be, just visit a surgical ward. Or a homeless shelter. Or a battered women's center. There's nothing like seeing someone else's problems to put yours in perspective.

- Remember what God has done for you. He gave you the ultimate sacrifice: His Son on a cross. Salvation. Eternal life. Quote John 3:16 to nudge your recall.

- Remind yourself who God is. He's the Creator of the very world around you, the air that you breathe, the heart that faithfully beats in your chest even when you worry it may break in two. He's bigger than your problems, wiser than your creditors, stronger than your fears, and more than able to multiply your resources—if you turn them over to Him. Remember the poor widow in 2 Kings 4:1–7? Pull out your Bible and reread that passage right now. Notice that God used the little bit of oil she had—her only real asset—to produce a miracle that literally saved her family. The God of the Bible is the same God of today—He's the same yesterday, today, and tomorrow. There is no statute of limitations on miracles.

- Keep serving others. Even if you feel that you're the one needing service. "God is not unjust. He will not forget how hard you have worked for him and how you have shown your love to him by caring for other believers, as you still do" (Hebrews 6:10 NLT). Give of yourself to the poor or needy even when you think you don't have anything to give. You do. The best blessing you can give someone is your time. Use your downtime to bless someone else. You might be surprised at how quickly downtime turns into uptime (see Hebrews 6:11–12).

- Keep your eyes fixed on Jesus. Yes, it's hard—incredibly hard—but it is possible. Do the things you know you need to do to honor your Savior, even if you don't feel like it. "Look straight ahead, and fix your eyes on what lies before you" (Proverbs 4:25 NLT). Go to church, hang out with believers, study your Bible, listen to Christian music. . .because feeding our faith starves our fears.

- You're not just a survivor. You're a conqueror. No, you're even more than that! "We are more than conquerors through him that loved us" (Romans 8:37 KJV). Now hold your head up and begin acting like you're on the winning side.

It's Not Over Till You Win

If you're walking through the valley of financial death right now, my heart goes out to you. I understand better than you think. My family crossed that lonesome valley, too. We went through a very rough patch when the kids were small—and oh, so expensive. My husband's full-commission, insurance sales job combined with my occupational therapy income just wasn't enough to cover all the bills.

I know all too well that ominous darkness that seizes your heart when official-looking men with clipboards appear at the door, or when your electricity is turned off, or when you want to fling the ringing phone against the wall because you know it's another bill collector. And you've run out of answers when your kids don't understand why they can't go places and do the same things their friends do. And you're bone tired. And more discouraged than you've ever been in your life.

I really do know, sister. And I want to offer you hope. Because I also know that there's life after financial death. Hope is what you need more than anything. Hope looks forward; regret looks back; anxiety looks everywhere at once. Cling to hope, dear one. Because fear is devoid of hope and hope is devoid of fear. Yielding to fear is like dying little deaths over and over until you really are. . .dead.

Remember, you're merely the caretaker; Papa God is the rightful owner of everything you consider yours, and if circumstances beyond your control remove it from your possession, He knows. He cares. And He has something special for you just beyond the next bend in the road.

You, too, can be a Lazarus. Like Georgia says, it's not over until you win. Fear is a huge, black hole, devouring your spirit and keeping you entombed. One day when you least expect it, you're going to hear a booming voice calling from the mouth of your tomb, "Come forth" (John 11:43 KJV).

So get ready to shuck your grave clothes and hustle your fanny right outta there. There's a bright new world waiting for you.

*Avoiding danger is no safer in
the long run than outright exposure.
The fearful are caught as often as the bold.*

HELEN KELLER

More Pluck, Less Chicken

1. Has there been a time when you felt as though you were walking through the valley of the shadow of financial death? When?

2. What can you identify with most in Georgia's story?

3. Looking back on your life, when was a time of adversity that you now know was a necessary part of your maturing process?

4. Is it ever tempting for you to spit out bitter words when you feel someone has treated you badly or hurt you? What can you do to sweeten your words?

5. What does Romans 8:37 mean to you? Read it aloud and then ponder it a bit. How about taping this short, powerful verse to your mirror?

Chapter 18

Creaks in the Night
(Fear of the Unknown)

*True, they can kill you,
but then what can they do?
There's nothing they can
do to your soul.*

Luke 12:4 MSG

*T*he thud of hurried footsteps pounding the cabin's pine floorboards awakened me with a start. It was early—far too early for anyone to be up. My daughter Cricket, son-in-law Josh, and their five-week-old baby, Blaine, had accompanied me on a getaway to our Smoky Mountain cabin, and the early spring chill alone was enough to keep you snuggled in your quilt.

Somewhere in the house a door slammed. What was going on?

Suddenly, loud, panicked voices rent the darkness. As I jerked to my feet and hit the floor running, my frantic heart collided with my ribs and all I could think was, *The baby! Something's happened to the baby!*

But there, standing by the wide-open front door, yelling and stomping with all his might, was Josh, holding a perfectly fine but wide-eyed baby Blaine.

Confusion muddied my brain. Our remote mountain cabin

is surrounded by dense woods on all sides. What in the world was happening in the small clearing we called our front yard?

All at once, Cricket burst into the house, carrying a squealing, wriggling, blood-soaked fur ball. Dirt streaked Cricket's pajamas and her eyes welled with tears as she rushed toward the kitchen sink, trailing splotches of sticky blood on the floor behind her. I realized with a pang that she was carrying Rocky, their five-pound Russian toy terrier. As we worked to clean his wounds and assess the damage, a strange story emerged.

Josh had risen at 5:00 a.m. to feed baby Blaine, and Rocky, having accompanied them to the living room rocking chair, curled himself up at his master's feet. Then something suddenly raised Rocky's hackles. He jumped up and began yipping at the door. Josh, in his drowsy state, thought Rocky simply needed to go potty outside, so he got up and opened the front door.

Now at this point you must understand something important about Rocky. We're talking about a full-grown dog the size and temperament of a dwarf bunny. His own reflection renders him lily-livered. Everything intimidates the little guy. Wee Rocky-feller turns into a quivering pulp when a fly buzzes by. He's terrified of all animals and people who venture anywhere near him. I've seen him hightail it away from an earthworm, I kid you not.

So that fateful morning, when Rocky, the king of cowardice, detected strange forces that he apparently considered a threat to his family, he somehow dredged up enough courage to race out the door, down the deck steps, and straight into the deadly jaws of a pack of coyotes.

Although only the silhouettes of the German shepherd–sized predators were visible in the misty darkness before dawn, the vicious, snarling sounds of the attack were horrible. Josh, who didn't dare enter the fray with the baby in his arms, could only stomp and yell from the doorway in hopes of scaring them away.

Cricket was rousted from her bed by Josh's shouts and flew outside. At her approach, the coyotes skittered into the woods and our brave little hero was left bleeding in a heap of fur and bones. By the grace of God, Rocky suffered only a dislocated shoulder, several deep gashes, and multiple puncture wounds. The exact imprint of upper and lower teeth from a large jaw was embedded in his back and belly.

But it could have been a lot worse.

When Cricket later asked the veterinarian who treated Rocky if he saw many coyote attack victims from the mountains, his chilling reply was, "No. There's usually no victim left to see. Coyotes typically snatch their prey and run, even when they're being chased or shot at; nothing will stop them. It's completely uncharacteristic that they dropped your little dog before he was ripped to shreds."

Shudder. I wouldn't use the word *uncharacteristic*. . .I'd use the word *miraculous*.

Now I realize that Rocky isn't human, but I believe we can learn a lot from our furry friends. I've always taken stock in Job 12:7: "Ask the animals, and they will teach you" (NIV).

Little Rocky-muffin has fears—real, horrifying, heart-pounding, wet-your-pants fears—just like us. Fears that often overwhelm and incapacitate him. Just like us. Sometimes fright is elicited by what he sees, but in this case, his enemy was something he couldn't see. It was something he sensed. Just like us.

Facing the Faceless

So many times it's the unseen that scares the snot out of us. . . faceless fears, things not visible that strike terror in our heart. It may be irrational anxiety we just can't shake, things unfamiliar or changing in our lives, or those niggling worries that make our imaginations careen recklessly into the what-ifs. Sometimes it's vague shapes stealthily moving through the fog of our minds, or maybe frightening bogeymen that have lurked beneath our beds since childhood.

Yep. Things that creak in the night make us freak in fright. And it's been that way for centuries. Julius Caesar said, "As a rule, what is out of sight disturbs men's minds more seriously than what they see."

And once we start fretting about our faceless foes, we can't seem to stop. Fear of something is what gives it power. Without our fear to promote and empower it, the thing itself is neutral, even impotent. But it takes only a spark of worry to ignite a blaze of anxiety. Little fears beget bigger fears. And fear can be addictive once you've acquired a taste for it.

Caving in to the fantasy world of reticent, faceless apprehension only results in distrust, discontent, and joylessness. The old adage is so true: "Worry gives even the smallest thing a big shadow."

So how do we stop quivering over what's hiding in those shadows? There are so few monsters that truly deserve our shivers. What can neutralize the obscure, haunting, often nameless concerns that bedevil us? How do we strip them of the power they hold over us?

Well, we must first discover what causes us to worry so much about the unknown. Did something concealed during childhood eventually emerge to cause us pain? Have we been wounded so many times in the past that we're anxiously biding our time until some new evil blindsides us? Or maybe we're just fainthearted about failing. This self-reflection is crucial because fear diminishes as understanding increases.

Consider my niece Andie. After she was born with cerebral

palsy and severe visual impairment, Andie's childhood was shaped by frustrations beyond her control. The brain bleed that Andie sustained during her premature birth caused motor deficits (uncoordination) and produced lags in specific linear mental-processing skills such as computing numbers and expressing herself on paper.

Consequently, Andie developed a strong fear of failure and dreaded "looking stupid" when she couldn't perform adequately. During early adolescence, her three biggest fears were math, creative writing, and playing the drums. That last one sounds a bit funky, but because Andie loved rhythm so much, her parents bought her a drum set and offered to pay for lessons, thinking it might be therapeutic in developing better motor skills.

But Andie, now a twenty-two-year-old college student, wouldn't go near those drums. "I was petrified of screwing up and felt I could never be as good as others," Andie now confesses. She died a thousand deaths when required to write school essays or work algebra equations, too. It took her five times longer than everyone else, and she wrestled with an underlying inferiority complex.

Then when she turned fourteen, something changed. A huge fan of young adult fantasy fiction (via audio books because of complete blindness in one eye and legal blindness in the other), Andie discovered an online site called Fan Fiction where kids wrote their own endings to popular YA story prompts. Andie, who'd always had a stellar imagination (probably because she couldn't depend on her eyesight to amuse herself as a child), realized that she could come up with much more exciting adventures than most of those that the "normal" kids suggested, so she forced herself to face down her long-standing fear of failure and stay at the computer keyboard until she managed to peck out her ideas.

The barrage of positive reinforcement Andie received about her writing made her realize that perhaps she was wrong, too, about the other fears that were self-imposed roadblocks in her life. Maybe, just maybe, she'd built Mount Kilimanjaro out of a speed bump.

So she dusted off those terrifying drums and dove into lessons. Eight years later, drumming is one of the supreme joys of her life. She's played in praise bands and church services—excelling in a skill her doctors said she'd never be able to accomplish.

"God sure has a sense of humor," Andie quips about her three biggest fears becoming her biggest assets. She recently received the annual Mathematics Achievement Award from her junior college and is currently writing her first book while pursuing a major in English.

Living a bold, abundant, fulfilling life: that's what Andie's doing now, versus cowering before fearful, oppressive shadows. Which sounds more appealing to you?

The Bigger Picture

Fear of the unknown thrives on what we think could happen, not on reality. Author Theodore Vail said, "Real difficulties can be overcome; it is only the imaginary ones that are unconquerable." The more we speculate, the more we anticipate the worst our imaginations can contrive, realistic or not. It's like visiting London and never leaving your hotel room for fear of running into Jack the Ripper.

I'm actually a good (or bad) example. I find change extremely scary, so when I encounter it, I imagine the worst possible scenarios. Little changes, big changes, life-altering changes—anything outside my comfortable routine—causes me to resist, complain, weep, and often plant my feet and tug backward with all my might. I'm afraid I won't be able to adapt, that things will get worse instead of better (no matter how bad it was to begin with), that anything new or different will take more energy and effort than I can give. Change sounds just too, well. . . messy.

It's easy to lose sight of the bigger picture that Papa God uses changes—especially difficult changes—to draw us closer to Him. If we're too focused on our comfort level, we tend to make the easy decision rather than facing the potential discomfort of seeking the right one.

I'm reminded of the Old Testament children of Israel who were also chickenhearted about change. Time after time, as Moses was leading them away from their oppressive lives of Egyptian slave labor, they complained about having to adapt to the inconveniences of the journey. Moving forward into the unknown was more frightening than going back to their previous miserable but predictable existence. (See Exodus 16:3 and 17:3 for examples of their whining.)

In their cowardice, they did all sorts of stupid things— questioned God's power (after they'd just witnessed huge miracles, including the Ten Plagues and the parting of the Red Sea), disobeyed countless times, nearly stoned their deliverer, Moses, and built a golden calf to worship instead of Almighty God.

C'mon, now. Of all things to promote into deity: a cow.

I just can't get a thrill from worshipping a Holstein, can you?

Haunted by the What-Ifs

Yet still today, fear often causes us to run ahead of God like those Israelites, taking matters into our own hands rather than waiting on the Lord to act. "Wait for the LORD, and He will save you" (Proverbs 20:22 NASB). Instead of relaxing in that promise, we charge ahead into the fantasy world of the what-ifs, a source of ongoing fear—real and imagined—for many women.

Fretting over the what-ifs causes many a long, sleepless night as we sculpt features onto our faceless anxieties, effectively giving fear laser eyes, supersonic ears, and a cavernous mouth. The monster we've created first begins whispering legitimate concerns into our heart's ear but ends up shrieking alarming possibilities that could. . .just might. . .most likely. . .inevitably. . . will happen.

Do you remember the *I Love Lucy* episode when Lucy decides to bake her own bread? As she mixes and kneads the dough, a tiny pinch of yeast just doesn't seem like enough, so she dumps in more. Then she leaves the pans of dough to rise. When she returns, huge blobs of gooey, sticky bread dough have ballooned over the sides of the pans and are oozing to the floor.

That basically describes the what-ifs: über yeast. Only a pinch of runaway, negative, worst-case scenarios can balloon into heaping, globbing, overwhelming terror. The best way out is to recognize the fear-rising process when it begins and intervene by redirecting our thoughts to that which is optimistic, hopeful, and Christ-reflective. "Fix your thoughts on what is true, and honorable, and right" (Philippians 4:8 NLT).

In case you didn't notice, "true, and honorable, and right" are the opposite of untrue, and dishonorable, and wrong. Which is usually where the what-ifs lead us. Thankfully, we don't have to follow.

When fear jumps its creek bed and begins flooding the banks of your life, it's time to build a DAM.

D: Damage Control. Recognize the fear that's sabotaging you. Name it: "I'm afraid of pain. . .failure. . .cancer. . .the dark. . . ." Be specific. Give your fear a distinctive face.

A: Attach a bit. Like a bit controls a horse's direction, steer your thoughts toward victory over the image of your fear that you've pictured. Keep moving forward; don't stall out in defeat. Remember, you're not battling alone. You have help. Divine help. Every time your fear assaults you, default to a key scripture you've memorized (see chapter 16 for suggestions).

M: Manage your fear. Decide what you're going to do about combating your fear, then follow your plan. Make good choices in what you allow to influence you mentally, physically, and spiritually (the books and magazines you read, the movies you see, the people you listen to).

Speaking of people you listen to, have you noticed that fear of the unknown has the converse effect of shrinking God in your eyes and enlarging the opinions of others? Anxiety over your own loss of control often makes you turn to others for guidance rather than to the Shaper of your future.

It makes no sense, but you know it's true—how many times have you, frantic over a looming major decision, called your BFF rather than hit your knees? Or believed something you read in a magazine over what you read in the Bible?

Count me guilty on that one, too.

As I've said before and I'll say again, fear is really a control issue. We think if we can somehow maintain control over things that happen to us, we'll be able to cruise along in happiness, peace, and tranquility. No surprises. No unforeseen pain. No disappointments. But being in control is just an illusion. We may think we're in control, but the fact is, we've never been in control. And we never will be.

For some of us control addicts, that's the most frightening thought of all.

Fear Factor

I love Elisabeth Elliot's perspective on gripping too tightly to control: "Today is mine. Tomorrow is none of my business. If I peer anxiously into the fog of the future, I will strain my spiritual eyes so that I will not see clearly what is required of me now."

Face it, sister, you have no control over what creaks in the night, what others think of you, whether that other driver will start texting just as your daughter's car approaches, the longevity of your internal organs, the cruelty of the natural aging process, when your loved ones will be called to eternity, or a thousand other possibilities you can invent. You can't control what God does or doesn't do. Because He is God. He's the One in control. He always has been and always will be.

And your best fear factor is to trust Him. As my pastor, Mark Saunders, says, "The trusting Jesus download doesn't come with a fear app."

When our worst fears confront us, we face the same choices little Rocky did: fight, flight, freeze, or freak out. Which option will we choose? Will we take off, running willy-nilly without a plan except to be anywhere but here? Will fear immobilize us, disabling our ability to make decisions or think clearly? Will we simply scream and cover our heads until help arrives? Or will that mysterious supernatural courage from Papa rise up within us and empower us to put up our dukes. . .to take on a fight even when the odds are big-time against us?

A year after his near-fatal coyote encounter, Rocky still limps. I suppose he always will. It's a reminder to our family of the reality of God's grace when we're under fire. A living memo that even if we're small, and have sweaty paws and a liver that quivers at an earthworm, we can still find courage when we need it.

*I learned that courage was not the
absence of fear, but the triumph over it.
The brave man is not he who does not
feel afraid, but he who conquers that fear.*

NELSON MANDELA

More Pluck, Less Chicken

1. What is your biggest unseen fear—that faceless fear that keeps you awake at night, worrying? What would you consider the best possible resolution for this faceless fear? The worst-case scenario?

2. Review Luke 12:4, found at the beginning of this chapter. How does this verse apply to your worst-case scenarios? In what way does it change your perspective of the worst thing that could possibly happen to you?

3. Repeat the acronym DAM aloud: Damage control, Attach a bit, Manage your fear. How can you dam the flow of fear that threatens to overflow its creek bed in your life?

4. What's your usual first impulse when coming face-to-face with one of your fears: fight, flight, freeze, or freak out? Has your reaction changed with maturity?

5. How do the what-ifs act as yeast in enlarging your fears? Brainstorm two practical ways you can redirect your thoughts and apply Philippians 4:8.

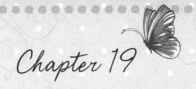

Chapter 19

Muzzling the Monster
(Death)

Where, O death, is your victory?
Where, O death, is your sting?

1 CORINTHIANS 15:55 NIV

❧

I knock softly. A gray-haired woman with smile-crinkled eyes answers the door and graciously invites me in. When I admire her lovely landscaped yard, she shyly admits that she's a master gardener and takes care of it herself.

Wow. You'd never know she was dying.

It's not that Jo Anne is unaware that she won't be here this time next year; it's just that she refuses to allow the cancer that's robbed her of an earthly future to stop her. She won't let the heartbreak of losing her beloved Bill after fifty-six years of marriage stop her. Nor will she allow major medical setbacks—including the recent loss of three fingers—to deter her from living. Every day. Every moment.

I so admire this lady. And I want to know her secret. How does she muzzle that bloodthirsty monster of fear stalking her in the shadows of the final path of life? What gives her the motivation to continue serving others even as she faces the certainty of her own numbered days?

"Well, I've not always had the peace I have today," Jo Anne admits. "It's a journey."

Jo Anne's journey began with anything but peace. For the first twenty-five of her seventy-eight years, she searched tirelessly for an unknown, unnamed something...something she couldn't find. She studied all the "isms"—Buddhism, Hinduism, Judaism, Confucianism. But the inner peace she sought eluded her. She struggled for years with chronic health issues and became, in her words, "so miserable and unhappy, I wanted to commit suicide. It wasn't because my body was sick; it was because my heart was sick."

Then one day, a minister's words resonated deep inside her. Jo Anne says, "It's not the why in life, it's the how. I realized there were no answers to all of my 'why' questions, but there were real answers to 'how.' I recognized that I didn't have the Lord Jesus in my heart, and once I turned my life over to Him, the 'hows' started making sense. I've been spiritually fulfilled ever since." Jo Anne finally found that peace she wanted so badly, and it saw her through dozens of military moves, constantly uprooting her two children, leaving friends and beloved churches behind, and starting over every few years.

Helping others became Jo Anne's personal mission. At one point, she grew restless with her limited options to serve in her traditional church. "I wasn't satisfied to just bake cookies for Sunday school anymore. It seemed that the church was teaching us to be deep-sea divers and then they'd have us pulling the plug out of the bathtub."

It was at that time Jo Anne became involved with Stephen Ministries, a cross-denominational service designed to match people walking through personal crises with Stephen Ministers trained to support, truly listen (sometimes for hours at a time), offer comfort, and basically stand by them through their time of need.

Jo Anne cites as an example the "very fearful lady" with severe cardiac issues whom Jo Anne supported by attending doctor's appointments with her, praying with and for her, and urging her to eat right and do her recommended exercises, even to the extent of accompanying her on walks. Jo Anne encouraged her on a nearly daily basis for six months, until the woman reached the point of physical and spiritual independence in her new healthy lifestyle.

Jo Anne continues to give others her time, now-limited energy, and prayers through the Stephen Ministry, even as she faces a time when she may soon need to be on the receiving end. Since a severe reaction to chemo drugs caused her to lose circulation in three fingers of her dominant right hand (they turned black and shriveled up as if frostbitten), Jo Anne has been unable to do the miniature landscaping or needlepoint art that she loves.

But she believes that joy can be found in all situations if you make the effort to look for it. Jo Anne asks herself each morning, "Where will the joy be today?" And she's never disappointed, virtually glowing as she tells me about a hummingbird that hovered six inches from her shoulder while she stood in her garden yesterday. She points out her backyard butterfly bushes that have attracted extra butterflies this year, which she believes is a special gift from her Lord to see her through these last days.

"One of the blessings of cancer," Jo Anne confides with a twinkle in her cornflower-blue eyes, "is that it makes people tell you they love you more often. So I'm constantly asking myself, 'Have I loved somebody well today? Have I shown someone that Jesus loves them?' It brings you out of your little cave to focus on others. During my years in the Stephen Ministry, I've seen too many people's lives shattered because they weren't loved enough. Everyone needs to know that even when people fail to love you, Jesus never will."

After caring for Bill, who combated heart problems for fifteen years before he passed away in 2007, Jo Anne makes the astounding statement, "Death doesn't scare me. I do worry about the pain related to dying sometimes, and I occasionally have my little temper tantrums, but I'm not going to waste my final time dwelling on the negative. No one wants to go through pain, but if there's no pain, there's no victory. Even Jesus had to endure the pain before His victory."

Making Love Your Legacy

Here are some heartfelt endurance suggestions from Jo Anne and other brave souls who are nearing the final strains of their last dance:

- Be an intentional blessing to someone. Devote yourself to caring for others. Even when your own needs begin to dominate your attention, set aside time daily to tune in to others. Pray for their specific needs and speak blessings to those you encounter each day. Make them glad they met you.

- Seek joy. Each morning ask yourself, "Where will the joy be today?" and then look for it. Look high and low—in misty sunbeams, your favorite poem, the kind eyes of your caretaker, dew-touched spiderwebs, fluffy white clouds scuttling by, even extra butterflies summoned by heaven just to make you smile.

- Prepare love notes. When energy permits, write, videotape, or audiotape little messages of encouragement to children, grandchildren, and friends for special occasions in their

future. Reminders of your love when you won't be there
to tell them yourself. Enlist the help of a friend or family
member to present your messages at the right time, labeled,
"For my granddaughter on her wedding day," "For my beloved friend's sixty-fifth birthday," or "For my dear son and
daughter-in-law on their golden anniversary."

- Pass on your faith. Purchase a supply of Bibles and in the
front flap of each one, write a personal dedication to the
child or grandchild, friend, or neighbor you intend to give
it to. Choose a specific book of the Bible (the Gospels are a
great place to start) and read several chapters daily, writing
comments in the margin of how this verse impacted your
life or what that verse means to you. Include personal notes
or prayers for the recipient related to highlighted scriptures. Your words will become a precious keepsake of faith
for generations to come. (*Helpful hint: A Bible with this
idea in mind might make a thoughtful gift for a loved one
standing at the threshold of eternity. Not only will it immerse the person in the comforting balm of scripture, but
it will give him or her a very worthwhile project that will
long benefit those he or she loves.)

- Make love your legacy. Emily Dickinson said, "Unable
are the loved to die. For love is immortality." Ask yourself,
"What will people remember most about me?" Meditate
on John 15:12: "Love each other as I have loved you" (NIV).
Tape it beside your bed so it's the last thing you see at
night and the first thing you see in the morning.

- "Remember that God loves you and will see you through
it." This is the primary message Jo Anne wants to share
with you about transitioning to the final frontier: hope.
Wrap your arms and legs around hope and cling to the

promise of heaven. This earth and all of its sorrows will pass away, but heaven is forever.

Death leaves a heartache no one can heal;
love leaves a memory no one can steal.

ENGRAVED ON AN IRISH HEADSTONE

*Jo Anne departed Earth for her forever home in heaven eight weeks after this interview.

More Pluck, Less Chicken

1. Jo Anne mentions an internal "cave" that terminally ill people tend to crawl into. Do you know someone languishing in such a dark, cold, isolated place? What is one thing you could do to help him or her emerge from his or her cave?

2. What are two special personal joys that you can share with someone who is ill? A beloved photograph? A happy memory? An uplifting poem or scripture? A handful of cheerful flowers? Singing or playing his or her favorite song or hymn?

3. Consider writing a love letter to your ill loved one detailing "five reasons you are special to me." Hand-draw little hearts or symbols of love to show how much you care; include photos if available to lavish love upon that person during his or her time of greatest need to feel loved.

4. Have you ever asked yourself, "If I found out today that I was dying, do I truly trust that Papa God would carry me through it?" If so, what was your response?

5. Reread the last paragraph of this chapter. Do you have that hope that Jo Anne was talking about?

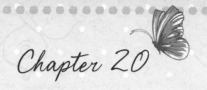

Chapter 20

Toxic Voices
(Detox for Negative Self-Talk)

*I have learned in whatever
state I am, to be content.*

PHILIPPIANS 4:11 NKJV

❦

$\mathcal{A}$ few years ago, while speaking at an elegant women's tea at a large metropolitan church, I casually mentioned that I had lost forty pounds the previous year. It wasn't something I'd planned to say—it just slipped out while I was making another point.

After I finished speaking, several ladies approached me to chat. One was a woman with impeccable makeup, in her early sixties, wearing an expensive tailored outfit with her fluffy hair perfectly coiffed.

"Why, Debora," she said in a charming Southern drawl, "I just want to thank you for sharing with us today. I think it's simply wonderful that you lost all that weight. I do have a question for you." She paused as a coy smile lifted the corners of her luscious berry-blush lips.

Why did I have a sudden premonition that something wicked this way cometh?

"Tell me," she almost purred, eyeing me up and down, "how long do you think it'll be before all that loose skin starts to shrink back up?"

Yes, this really happened, and no, I don't know why some people think that by blowing out someone else's candle their own burns brighter. My point is that we get enough negativity from the world; we don't need to pile any more on ourselves.

But that's exactly what we do when we listen to those toxic voices droning inside our heads. As I said in my book *Too Blessed to Be Stressed,* when channeling Eeyore becomes the soundtrack for our subconscious thoughts, those mopey, self-depreciating donkey thoughts can wear us down and wear us out before we even realize the source of erosion. (Check out the chapter called "Can I Hear Me Now?" in *Too Blessed to Be Stressed* for some great practical tips on overdubbing negative self-talk.)

By allowing our corrosive inner soundtrack to rattle on—by not muting the volume and changing the channel—we're at high risk of becoming slaves to our own emotions. We think we can control them, but we can't. We underestimate the persuasive power of persistent voices like outrage, distrust, jealousy, resentment, bitterness, and revenge. They are such strong, emotive voices that we can't ignore them.

Caving to the Voices

The Bible has many examples of people who caved to their toxic inner soundtrack. Let's look at a few.

Saul, the tall, handsome donkey herder who was God's handpicked choice as the first king of Israel, repeatedly refused to obey the Almighty and was eventually rejected by the same hand that had crowned him (see 1 Samuel 16:1). God's Spirit left Saul and he was filled with depression and fear (see 1 Samuel 16:14).

Whoa. Let's stop right there for a moment and take note of what happens when disobedience separates us from the Spirit of the Lord. . .we are filled with depression and fear. This is a crucial point. Swipe it with your highlighter.

Now back to our story. The toxic voices of depression and fear began dogging Saul, jeering at him with a bitter rasp of jealousy over David, the young shepherd boy turned giant-slayer who had been employed as a palace musician. Then one day as David was strumming his harp to soothe the king, those inner voices rose to fever pitch and "Saul hurled his spear at David. But David dodged out of the way, and leaving the spear stuck in the wall, he fled and escaped into the night" (1 Samuel 19:10 NLT).

David's Jackie Chan move was the beginning of the end for Saul, for he severed his relationship with the future king (David), Saul's own son Jonathan, and the people over whom he reigned. Saul lost his kingdom and his life because he chose to believe those toxic voices.

Listening to his inner voice of anger caused Jonah to run off by himself, curl up under a big leafy plant, and pout like a spoiled little boy who broke his favorite Tonka truck when he didn't get his way. After Jonah had reluctantly shouted a message of impending doom up and down the streets of Nineveh, God mercifully changed His mind about destroying the repentant city, but "this change of plans greatly upset Jonah, and he became very angry. So he complained to the LORD about it" (Jonah 4:1–2 NLT).

I can just picture irate, fish-reeking, glowering Jonah throwing his sweaty mantle into the dirt and shaking his walking stick toward heaven. "Just kill me now, LORD! I'd rather be dead than alive if what I predicted will not happen" (Jonah 4:3 NLT).

From Jonah's perspective, it was all about him—saving face, avoiding humiliation, being right—rather than about the thousands of people whose lives had just been spared. He was focusing on the hole and missing the doughnut.

In all honesty, I have to admit that there have been times

when I've felt a lot like Jonah. . .so all about me and fearful of appearing foolish or just plain wrong that even death sounded more appealing. "Just shoot me," I'd rail, at the mercy of my inner self-pity voice. "Just shoot me now!"

Have you been there, too? Sometimes our selfish voices drive us to the edge of the cliff and throw us right out of the moving vehicle.

As for other examples, let's not forget Peter, who, upon seeing Jesus walking toward his storm-tossed boat across the face of the open sea, impetuously asked to join Him. "Yes, come," Jesus replied (Matthew 14:29 NLT). So over the side of the boat Peter went. I can just imagine the amazement and awe registering on his face when he landed on the sloshy surface, keeping his vision glued to the Maker of Miracles just a few yards away. Heart pounding, he took one incredible step. Then another. But suddenly the inner voices started—at first only whispering: *What are you doing, dude? You're not good enough to do this. You're not worthy of walking in Jesus' footsteps on land, much less on water.*

Then Peter took his eyes off Jesus and began wildly vacillating between the blustery wind whipping his robe around him and the white-capped waves crashing over his feet. All at once he could feel the coldness of the water, smell the brine of the deep. Peter moved his focus off Jesus and onto his circumstances. The toxic inner voices cranked up louder. *This is impossible! Are you out of your mind? No man can walk on water— you're going to drown, you fool!*

"He was terrified and began to sink. 'Save me, Lord!' he shouted. Jesus immediately reached out and grabbed him. 'You have so little faith,' Jesus said. 'Why did you doubt me?' " (Matthew 14:30–31 NLT).

"Why did you doubt Me?" That's the million-dollar

question, isn't it? Why do we doubt Him when He's standing there in the middle of our sea of tribulation, proving to us that He's more than powerful enough to rise above the storm and hold us up there with Him? Why does it feel so much safer to crawl back into the boat?

Because we choose to listen to our toxic inner voices and become a boat-hugger when we could be a water-walker.

And then there's Martha, kindred spirit of production-driven women everywhere. The just-get-it-done girls. Are you one of us? If so, you've heard the same toxic voices Martha did, and you know how convincing they can be.

Oh, our girl started out well (don't we all start out with good intentions?). In a gush of hospitality, she invited Jesus into her home for dinner. That was good. Ten points for Martha.

But as she hastily scribbled her grocery list, filled pots to boil, and started peeling mounds of potatoes, Martha frantically searched around for some help. Counting the twelve disciples, her own family, and various other followers in Jesus' entourage, she was probably planning food for at least twenty people. That's a lot of potatoes.

So she spotted her younger, prettier, more popular, apple-of-Daddy's-eye sister, Mary, sitting comfortably at Jesus' feet, soaking in His every word. (Okay, so I made up that description of Mary, but that's the way I've always imagined Martha's perception of her sister.)

Enter Martha's toxic inner voices: *Are you kidding me? Who does she think she is—the queen of Sheba? Why do I always have to do all the work and never get any appreciation for it? It's high time someone else took some responsibility around here.*

Sound familiar, girlfriend? Sure does to me. I think my inner voices and Martha's are cousins.

"Martha was distracted by the big dinner she was preparing. She came to Jesus and said, 'Lord, doesn't it seem unfair to you that my sister just sits here while I do all the work? Tell her to come and help me'" (Luke 10:40 NLT).

Now, at first glance, I leap to Martha's side on this one. Because I've been there and I totally get her indignation—everyone ignoring the server seems unjust. Completely unfair. Doesn't anybody care about me? I'm trying to do something nice, and I'm abandoned here sitting naked on an iceberg.

As Jesus points out, this scenario is worth a second look. It is an iceberg and there's more beneath the surface.

"But the Lord said to her, 'My dear Martha, you are worried and upset over all these details! There is only one thing worth being concerned about. Mary has discovered it, and it will not be taken away from her'" (Luke 10:41–42 NLT).

Jesus recognizes Martha's ruffled feelings—and in doing so, validates that based on what's visible here, being upset is not an unrealistic response. But at the same time, He points out that emotions are not trustworthy. They're blocking Martha's view of the real issues. Provision for her guests is important, certainly, and so is respectful assistance from her family, but there are things—nonphysical, can't-touch-this things—even more important here: spiritual health, discovery of truth, relationships, salvation of your very soul. Things that need to be rated on an eternity continuum, not a daily checklist.

Souls, after all, are infinitely more important than potato soufflé.

That's something I need to remember the next time my grumplitude shoots off the charts when the Hamburger Helper burns because my neighbor needs a sympathetic ear to vent about her day.

Antidote for the Poison

*O*kay, let's recap the emotions that triggered toxic voices in our four biblical examples:

- Jealousy
- Anger
- Irritation
- Fear
- Ingratitude
- Exasperation
- Inferiority
- Rage
- Selfishness
- Anxiety
- Abandonment
- Envy
- Being misunderstood
- Insecurity
- Indignation
- Mistrust
- Needing to be right
- Resentment
- Depression
- Frustration
- Feeling unappreciated
- Being emotionally spent
- Feeling disrespected
- Doubt
- Embarrassment

Do any of these feelings trigger negative voices inside you? Don't all of them? I think each of us struggles to stifle the destructive messages elicited by strong emotions. Let's take a look at some detox lessons we can learn from Saul, Jonah, Peter, and Martha.

In modern-day terms, Saul bit the hand that fed him. He completely forgot the piles of donkey poo he used to slog through in his pre-king days and neglected to be thankful for his blessings. He became self-centered and self-sufficient, no longer acknowledging the One responsible for his undeserved majesty, power, and lofty position. And worst of all, Saul grieved the heart of God by his willful disobedience (see 1 Samuel 15:11).

A fresh perspective of gratitude would have changed everything. Humility walking hand-in-hand with thankfulness likely would have created a desire within Saul to be obedient—and grateful—to the Source of his good fortune.

Peter, who desperately needed assurance of his Lord's sovereignty in his crucial moment of doubt, would have done well to remember the incredible miracles he had already witnessed Jesus perform. Why, Jesus had just fed five thousand people with a handful of bread and two wee fishes that very afternoon! How could Peter possibly doubt the supernatural power of Jesus as he stood before Him like a life-sized cork?

But he did.

How can we possibly doubt Jesus' power after all the miraculous heart transformations we've seen Him accomplish?

But we do. Even with a lifetime of evidence before us. Because fear is like static that keeps us from hearing our faith voices. All we can pick up are those destructive, devilish, poisonous voices that cast doubt on what we know to be true.

We obviously need to tune our receivers better. But how?

We could all (Peter, you, and I) benefit from a prayer journal—a wonderful way to chronicle Papa God's power in our lives. So when doubt assaults our faith, fear threatens to devour us, and disaster hovers overhead like a cyclone, we'll be able to instantly recall the times when Papa God's merciful hands rescued us in astounding ways. We'll develop miracle memory.

Having treated athletes in physical therapy clinics for over thirty years, I know something about how repetition of specific movement creates muscle memory. That's how pitchers learn to hit the inside corner, gymnasts land a back tuck precisely on a four-inch balance beam, and pianists memorize twenty-page concertos. Muscle memory. Practice, practice, and more practice establishes an instantaneous default system for muscles—they automatically "know" what to do in a specific circumstance because they've done it so many times before.

Listen, girlfriend, it's the same principle in dealing with fear. By remembering what Papa God has already done for us through Christ, we'll develop miracle memory. He's defeated the instigator of fear at the cross, and He'll do it again. And again. And again. With practice, our miracle memory will kick in, and we'll automatically default to faith rather than fear when difficulties come our way.

Jonah? Well, ol' Jonah just needed to BARF. I'm going to borrow a page from my book *More Beauty, Less Beast* and share my dirty little secret that really, truly works for exerting self-control when you feel your inner ogre clawing up your windpipe, all ready to lame, maim, and destroy. When you get angry enough to BARF, do it!

B: Back off—Walk away to gain a new perspective.

A: Admit—Identify your emotions in order to deal with them.

R: Redirect—Refocus your emotions in a healthier direction.

F: Forgive—First forgive your offender and then forgive yourself.

What about Martha? Who among us hasn't felt unappreciated? How many times just this week have you felt taken for granted? (That's a rhetorical question—you can stop counting them up now.)

But we have to remember that our worth comes from Christ; it's not dependent on how other people treat us. I love this statement I saw on a plaque: I MAY NOT BE PERFECT, BUT JESUS THINKS I'M TO DIE FOR. So true. We are exquisitely precious in the sight of our Lord, treasured beyond measure. And in the end, that value is the only kind that counts.

So when the next lady points out our Dumbo arm flaps and saggy, baggy thigh-u-lite, we can mute that toxic inner voice shouting at us to yank her Victoria's Secret panties into a major wedgie, and simply smile.

Because we know we're to die for.

Listen to what you know
instead of what you fear.

RICHARD BACH

More Pluck, Less Chicken

1. Do you ever struggle with the toxic voices of depression and fear like Saul? In which seasons of your life have you been plagued by these voices most?

2. Can you recall a time when you, like Jonah, had the perspective, "It's all about me"? What effect did that perspective have on your inner voices?

3. When has fear made you a boat-hugger rather than a water-walker?

4. Take another look at the list of strong emotions in this chapter. Which of these produces the most toxic voices for you? The least?

5. When have you been angry enough to BARF lately? Review the meaning of the acronym so that next time you'll be ready to regurgitate productively: B: Back off, A: Admit, R: Redirect, F: Forgive.

Chapter 21

Flip On the Light
(The Bogeyman's Busted)

*Everything exposed by
the light becomes visible.*

Ephesians 5:13 NIV

❧

*I*t's out there. Or maybe it's in here. In your closet or beneath your bed. Hiding. Watching. Waiting. Do you feel it stalking you? Biding its time, sharpening its claws, just waiting for you to lay your worry-weary self down and close your unsuspecting eyes in a futile attempt to sleep.

I'm talking about the frightening bogeyman whose DNA is loss. We've already talked about the fear of losing possessions, financial stability, friends, looks, health, self-esteem, and even life itself.

But there's one more monster. And it's huge.

Fear of losing a child, spouse, or parent was ranked number one by a sizable margin on my fear survey. Fifty-one percent of all women polled rated this simmering fear among their top three. I must admit I'm one of them.

Author Philip Gulley said, "Fear can keep us up all night long, but faith makes one fine pillow." I'm ashamed to say there have been times when I've opted to rest my head on the prickly cactus of fear rather than the comforting pillow of faith.

The horrifying possibility of losing precious loved ones looms large. Since the birth of my children, I've spent countless hours sweating out worst-case scenarios that, thankfully, never happened. Now that my parents are in their eighties, I fret about how I'll ever go on without them. When my husband's away, I worry about receiving that phone call that would drive me to my knees and possibly out of my mind.

According to Corrie ten Boom, "Worry is a cycle of inefficient thoughts whirling around a center of fear." Man, I know that tornado well. I've spent many a night whirling my sheets into knots as the worries in my head spin out of control. And apparently I'm not alone. You ride that twister, too, don't you?

But when all's said and done, it comes down to this: Would you rather be a frayed knot or afraid not?

Yes, sister, again it's our choice.

Think about it this way: Have you ever given someone a special gift that you spent significant time, energy, and money on because you just knew it would be perfect for them? Maybe you even sacrificed in order to purchase it because you wanted to demonstrate your warmest feelings by this awesome present.

My friend Annie did just that. Finances were tight, but after much soul-searching, Annie emptied her long-saved-up stash to purchase a $125 designer purse for her daughter-in-law for Christmas. Annie actually did without some things she needed for herself in order to show affection and acceptance of her son's new wife by this very special gift. Four months later, Annie found out (quite by accident) that her daughter-in-law had sold the purse at a yard sale for ten dollars.

I don't know about you, but that really makes my underwire burn. What a slap in the face! Disrespecting the gift disrespects the giver. What kind of insensitive clod would callously overlook the caring and self-sacrifice that went into such a special gift, and basically toss it away?

Yet you and I are at risk of doing the same thing when we allow fear to denigrate the incredible gift that we've been given—the gift of living freely and happily in the joy of the Lord. It's a gift that's already bought and paid for.

I surely don't want to waste any more of my precious life-moments because I stubbornly refuse to open my gift from Jesus. I want that freedom. I dream of that happiness. I crave that joy.

Don't you?

But as long as we continue to cower in fear, the precious gift that you and I have been offered by the sacrifice Jesus made for us when He exchanged His life for ours is reduced to, well, gum on the sole of our Nike. Something we scrape off and throw away.

Instead of living unfettered, we anxiously calculate every risk. Freedom disintegrates into shackles. Happiness is trounced by cowardice. Joy is replaced by angst. Instead of moving forward in boldness, we hold back in timidity.

Living in fear is not really living at all.

Still, that beautiful, perfect, specially chosen gift tied with the sparkly ribbon is waiting for us to unwrap and enjoy. "For God has not given us a spirit of fear and timidity, but of power, love, and self-discipline" (2 Timothy 1:7 NLT).

Let's face it: Losing a loved one is a legitimate concern that will, sadly, happen to each of us at some point in our lives. But through Papa God's gift of power, love, and self-discipline, we don't have to be consumed by the threat of loss. Throwing away a priceless present like joy-filled freedom from fear is a slap in the face to the One who purchased it for us with His love.

Unlike Annie's daughter-in-law, we don't want to disrespect the Giver by disrespecting the gift.

Sure, the bad things we imagine might happen. Sometimes they do happen. Such is life. But is it better to shoot out our own lights and crawl under the covers in anticipation of nightfall, or dance in the sunlight and deal with the darkness when the sun goes down?

My friend Esther was plunged into darkness after losing her three-year-old son, Adam, to cancer. Paralyzing fear blocked her escape from the blackness that progressively seeped into her soul. Her strength was drained as surely as if a hole had been punched in her heart, making her unable to flee the darkness or to reach up to flip on the light.

Seeing no way out of her despair, Esther attempted to take her own life. But Papa God intervened and, in His mercy, lit a candle in her darkness. The single flame gradually grew in warmth and intensity until a mighty blaze of light filled Esther with hope and strength and the will to live.

Looking back on her time in the darkness, Esther says, "Satan's number one strategy is to steal, kill, and destroy [see John 10:10]. When my new career took off [several years before Adam was diagnosed with cancer at age two], I just didn't have any energy left for things of God. In that loss of will, I grew spiritually weak over time, and Satan was able to do his worst. By the time Adam died, I had no strength left at all."

And the result was a fear-filled woman languishing in darkness.

After such a shattering loss, fear of losing her only other child began to control her thoughts. "It took several years for me to get over the raw emotions," Esther admits, "and another two decades before I could fully comprehend that 'if the Son makes you free, you will be free indeed'" (John 8:36 NASB).

It's that freedom we all want more than anything, isn't it? Freedom from the darkness of fear. Freedom from the threat of loss lurking at the edges of our minds. Freedom to throw our arms out wide as we live and laugh and love.

In order to find that freedom and effectively quench the darkness, we have to make the effort to reach upward toward the Source of all light and flip on the switch. Flood the room with light. Papa God's light. No bogeymen hanging out here! For God and fear cannot coexist in the same place; where His light shines, darkness vanishes. Fear is expelled by power, love, and self-discipline.

When the Lord's light penetrates the darkness of fear, according to Esther, "there is restoration of a life that has been turned upside down. No matter how low you go, you can still hear His voice if you listen for it. And if you can hear His voice, you can follow it out of the darkness."

The journey out of fear's darkness is certainly not easy. Not at all. Especially when our eyes have grown accustomed to the dark and we forget how much we need the light. We have to prod ourselves to remember that the way to start a journey of miles is by taking a single step. Pick up your right foot, move it forward three inches, put it down. Then repeat with your left foot.

And as we agreed back in chapter 18, change is scary. No matter how much it's needed and no matter how much we desire it. My friend, author Sharron Cosby, puts it well: "Fear is my security blanket. It's tattered and worn, but it's comfortable—something I know well."

It's tough to discard that ratty old blankie, even though a brand-new plush throw sits on your shelf.

What about the times when we have no choice? The times when, grope as frantically as we might, we just can't seem to find the light switch? The times when, because of circumstances beyond our control, we must remain in the darkness a little longer?

That's when we need a change of perspective. We must put on

our night-vision goggles so that we can see through the darkness and not be afraid. The bottom line, I think, is that we need to feel safe. Security is what makes the difference in how much the darkness affects us. I've got a swell story to illustrate this.

Earnest P. Squirrel was a tiny, nearly hairless baby squirrel that I rescued from the drooling jaws of death when my cat was preparing to have rodent pizza for lunch one day. When we weren't feeding Earnest cat's milk (oh, the irony!) with an eyedropper, he liked nothing better than to curl up in my pocket. He would stay there in the dark, rolled into a little ball, contentedly snoozing for hours at a time while I rode my bike, worked around the house, and even once forgot he was there and wore him to work at the hospital.

(Not a good idea, let me tell you. Especially when Earnest emerged from his nap and began leaping from patient to patient, searching for his dinner eyedropper. Can you say mass hysteria?)

Anyway, back to my point. Darkness doesn't have to be frightening. To Earnest, darkness was comforting—a cozy den that made him feel safe and secure. Because he trusted the one who put him there (the one who controlled the eyedropper, the source of his sustenance), he wasn't afraid of the darkness. Not to wax too anthropomorphically, but Earnest knew he was being taken care of, and his faith in his caretaker cast an entirely different perspective on the darkness. To him the blackness wasn't harsh, cold, or alarming. No, it was soft, warm, and welcoming—like ebony velvet.

Isn't ebony velvet the way you'd like to perceive the darkness, too?

I know, I know. Believe me, I do. It's awfully difficult to trust our Caretaker when we have experienced—or know someone who has experienced—devastating loss. Like Esther, we just can't understand and end up asking the hardest of unanswerable questions: Why? Why?

But the thing is, God's sovereignty is innately mysterious; He has the right to be unexplainable and unfathomable. He is God. I have this verse taped to my bathroom mirror to remind me of this: "The secret things belong to the LORD our God" (Deuteronomy 29:29 NIV).

Although death and loss are part of the cycle of life, Papa God's love for us remains strong and present. And where He is present, fear cannot be. So flip on the light. Watch the bogeyman hightail it out of there.

> *Don't fear change.*
> *Change fear.*
> UNKNOWN

More Pluck, Less Chicken

1. Are you one of the 51 percent who struggles with fear of losing a loved one? If so, when did that bogeyman first begin stalking you?

2. It's been said that fear and regret are the twin thieves that rob us of today. Do you find that true in your life? What can you do to foil the robbers?

3. Have you ever had someone disrespect a gift you gave them? How did it make you feel?

4. Reread 2 Timothy 1:7. Which packages (power, love, and self-discipline) that make up this special gift from Papa God have you unwrapped and used? Which have you yet to open? How do you think that makes Him feel?

5. During times when you can't find the light switch, do you perceive the darkness surrounding you as terrifying blackness or ebony velvet?

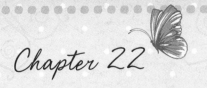

Chapter 22

Grit, Gumption, and Godiva
(Wrap-Up)

With his love, he will calm all your fears.

ZEPHANIAH 3:17 NLT

❧

*S*o what are you thinking now that you've stepped up and yanked the mask off some of your fear monsters? Are you surprised at what you found hiding underneath?

I hope you're recognizing a few things about fear: that fear isn't part of the Christ package. . .faith is. That worry is the result of putting your faith in the wrong place—in yourself (instead of Papa God) to figure it all out, maintain control, and provide protection from what might harm you. And that tolerating your fear monsters only makes them growl louder.

Confrontation is the only way to silence those bullying beasts.

My prayer for you is that you'll not remain fearified, but will instead be fortified by your chain mail Thanks-Spanx and custom-designed armor to morph into Xena, the Warrior Princess. And that you'll stay fortified by the grit, gumption, and Godiva you share with strong girlfriends sword-fighting in the trenches right alongside you. We're in this together, sister; and although one soldier may falter, there's incredible power in battalions.

Take heart! In your armor, you're one big, bad, bold, behunkus-whipping mama.

And don't you forget it.

Notes

1. Sherry Turkle, "Connected, but Alone?" TED.com, youtube/ +7xr3AsBEK4.

2. Statistics from LiveScience.com: http://www.livescience .com/13434-phobias-fears-acrophobia-heights-agoraphobia- arachnophobia.html.

3. "Cookies Lead to Assault, Deputies Say," *Tampa Tribune*, February 23, 2011.

4. "Obese Women Can't Avoid Media's Stigma," LiveScience. com, November 13, 2011.

5. "Half of America Has Sugary Drink Daily, CDC Says," *Tampa Tribune*, September 1, 2011.

6. "Weight Regain Might Be Biological," *Tampa Tribune*, October 29, 2011.

7. "Lab Rats Show Scientists Their Best Behavior," *Tampa Tribune*, December 9, 2011.

8. Dawn Hollomon, "Choose Forgiveness," *Home Life Magazine*, September 2011, 60.

9. "Iranian Blinded by Acid Spares Attacker," *Tampa Tribune*, August 1, 2011, section 2:1.

10. Bill Kirby, "A Hero among Heroes Who Sought Forgiveness," *Tampa Tribune*, November 11, 2011, 16.

11. "Youth Breaks Disease Norms," *Tampa Tribune*, April 1, 2012.

12. Centers for Disease Control and Prevention, cdc.gov.

13. "25% of Women Victimized," *Tampa Tribune*, December 15, 2011.

Visit with the Author

$\mathcal{D}$eb would love to chat with you and even share a few nuggets of truth gift-wrapped in humor with your church or women's group. Befriend her on Facebook and Twitter, and keep in touch through her website and blogs found at www.DeboraCoty.com.

Debora M. Coty is a popular speaker, columnist, lifelong Bible student, internationally published freelance writer, and award-winning author of numerous books, including *Too Blessed to Be Stressed* and *More Beauty, Less Beast*. She's also an orthopedic occupational therapist, writing instructor, and tennis addict. Mother of two grown children, Debora lives and loves in central Florida with her husband, Chuck, and desperately wicked pooch, Fenway.